Thorns
in the
Heart

Steven Stiles

CHRISM

Springfield, Missouri
02-0347

Chrism books are published by Gospel Publishing House.

Library of Congress Cataloging-in-Publication Data
Stiles, Steven, 1947–
    Thorns in the heart: a Christian's guide to dealing with pain / Steven Stiles.
      p.   cm.
    ISBN 0-88243-347-4
    1. Pain—Religious aspects—Christianity. 2. Consolation.
I. Title.
BV4909.S75   1994
248.8'6—dc20   94-8613

Printed in the United States of America

To all who suffer with pain
May God use this book to help them
find their way to recovery.

Table of Contents

Foreword

Some books are special. They are inspired by God to address issues vital to the Christian world and the development of believers. This is one of those books. If I had the power to make it mandatory reading, I would, for *Thorns in the Heart* is destined to provoke debate and change many lives.

This timely work by Dr. Steven Stiles will help persons find a better understanding of themselves—their faith and emotions, their response to pain and circumstances, and their relationships with God and others. In addition, it will serve as a guide for those attempting to help others cope with emotional pain or addiction.

I have participated in writing, editing, and publishing more than thirty books. *Thorns in the Heart* is among the most important of those books. In these days of "quiet desperation," when individuals are confronted with excessive emotional stress and conflict, they need biblical answers.

Dr. Stiles' book candidly discusses issues relevant to every reader, but this book is far more than a treatise on the problems facing the human spirit. This is a book of hope. These pages will reveal biblical guidelines for dealing with pain, and they will challenge readers to respond to pain and conflict in a Christ-honoring way.

Every week I hear men, women, and teens cry out for help. Their stories are often heart-wrenching. They are facing family conflicts, financial woes, and addictions. Other times their pain revolves around a job or a physical illness. Whether it is on the telephone or at the altar following a church service, they simply long to share their pain with someone. They often wonder aloud if God is aware of their crisis. They wonder why they have to endure difficult situations. They wonder if their emotional pain is punishment from God. Fortunately, we now have a book,

Thorns in the Heart, that will provide biblical answers to their questions and offer professional guidance.

I have had the opportunity to write books with some great Christian leaders, for example, Mark Buntain and Demos Shakarian. They were servants fully committed to winning souls and helping people. Dr. Stiles is that same type of selfless man. He has devoted years to helping hurting people. Thus, there is no doubt this book was born out of his love for people and his desire to see them find comfort and contentment in a world of chaos.

HAL DONALDSON
President
ChurchCare, Inc.

Preface

I began investigating the problem of pain because after years of counseling people with a wide range of emotional problems and addictions, it became clear that many Christians do not have a healthy understanding of the role pain should play in their lives.

The stories in this book are based on actual cases. Except where permission has been granted, specific details and circumstances have been altered to afford anonymity for those involved and to render all cases unidentifiable.

One case involves a minister who committed adultery. After considerable prayer and thought, I decided to include this story. It is not my intent to impugn ministers. My point is that if a minister can become a victim of pain, other believers can as well.

For some, this book may be controversial. Christians have differing views of what pain is, where it comes from, and, especially, how believers should respond to it.

Every theory and premise in this book is based on biblical and scientific evidence. While there are no easy answers to the problem of pain, understanding why we hurt and how God wants us to respond can be a wonderful source of hope.

Pain makes our faith grow!

Acknowledgments

I would like to acknowledge first and foremost the Good Shepherd.

With special appreciation to

My wife Nancy and my boys Josh, Joel, Johnny, Steven, and William, who were very patient while I took time to write

My parents, Mervin and Beulah Stiles, and my sisters, Enid Bundy and Meg DeMers, for always backing me

My colleagues at Bethany College, the Certification Program in Addiction Counseling (CPAC), and New Life Center for their support

Kristine Waters, Cheryl Finch, Bob Pagett, Dr. Esther Matteson, Dr. Derrald Vaughn, Dr. Don Corzine, Matt Key, Hal Donaldson, and Dr. Ken Horn for their technical assistance

Ted Sands

My many friends who suffer from physical and emotional problems but continue to keep the faith

In memory of

Nina Foster
Beulah Sands
Dr. Bernard Ramm

I am grateful to countless others.

Part 1: The Problem of Pain

ONE

THE BUMPS AND
BRUISES OF LIFE

"I waited patiently for the Lord; he turned to
me and heard my cry."

—Psalm 40:1

ONE

The Bumps and Bruises of Life

Limits to Pain

The year was 1954. Beneath an awkward arrangement of mosquito netting in an Amazon jungle Francine, a Wycliffe Bible translator, worked intently over an ancient typewriter that seemed to almost pulsate in the dull, flickering glow of a nearby kerosene lamp.

Thousands of miles separated Francine from the comfort and security of her native homeland. She was facing the biggest adjustment of her life. Not only did she have the task of learning a new language and culture, but she was responsible for teaching reading skills, health care, and agriculture.

The stress was persistent. At any time an animal or hostile war party could attack from the surrounding cover of dense vegetation. And then there were the mosquitoes. Even under the netting Francine was covered with welts. The People, as the Indians called themselves, repeatedly expressed wonder that she had willingly joined them in their perpetual itching, pain, disease, fear, and hunger.

Though the stress was taking a heavy toll on Francine, she pressed toward her self-imposed deadline. She saw too many friends dying without God's Word in their language. The constant pressure turned to mental exhaustion. At day's end her body protested with aches and pains that seemed to join forces with her mental exhaustion. Francine found herself dreading the long walk across the village to her bedroll. Hut by hut, the dogs would lunge at her, snapping and snarling. What was normally quite troublesome loomed tonight as intolerable. She wondered if she really had the strength left to face the merciless dogs.

Blowing out the kerosene flame above the typewriter, she reluctantly turned in the direction of her hut. She took a deep breath and stepped into the darkness. From her heart arose a simple prayer, brief and furtive, too urgent to include any profound considerations: *Lord, the dogs, please.*

God answered. On the walk across the village, dog after dog raced at her, but they all stopped abruptly, their mouths never opening. One by one, they cowered and slunk silently away as if encountering a great upturned hand. It was strangely quiet. The only sounds came from deep within the jungle, for God had intervened to temporarily limit Francine's emotional and physical pain.

God is concerned about our pain. In His mercy He has placed natural limits on both our emotional and physical discomfort. Felt pain has to stop somewhere. This limit to pain is based on two facts. First, our nervous system can cope with only given amounts of pain at a time. Second, God has equipped us with an internal chemical system for combating both physical and emotional pain.

There is one other merciful limit to pain. At times God intervenes miraculously as He did with Francine. Only God can instantly heal bodies or silence dogs in the night; only God can stop the natural progression of pain.

God allows emotional and physical pain to have a precise and necessary influence in our lives. Pain is personalized. God knows how much we need and how much we can handle. We cannot function or survive when pain becomes too great. On the other hand, with too little pain we would not be motivated to survive at all! We must live in an uncomfortable balance. Stress brings us pain and in turn, pain helps us respond appropriately to stress. Although stress took a heavy toll on Francine, it also persuaded her to finally go to her hut to get some much needed rest.

Physical and Emotional Pain

Both our bodies and minds are stress sensitive. So much so, it would be hard to say whether Francine suffered more from physical or emotional pain, for they always intermingle. Both contributed to her discomfort and exhaustion. Both caused her to lean on God.

"*Kachinyehno, kachinyehno!*" ("Pain, it hurts me.") The wailing voice echoed through the sleeping village and shattered the quiet of early dawn. The People heard the noise far up the jungle clearing. Francine had been asleep only five and a half hours, but the urgency of the cry jolted her with adrenaline, and wrenched her into consciousness. There it was again. *"Kachinyehno."* It sounded like Tiri.

With a deep foreboding, Francine hurried toward the outcry. Others were already running in the same direction. *What could it be?* she thought. *Was Tiri sick? Had she fallen and broken a leg? Was she cut by a marauder's machete?* A few more steps and she knew the answer. There were no cuts or broken bones, not even a bruise. It was a massive wound to the soul. *"Kachinyehno,"* Tiri sobbed, "my husband has gone downriver with another woman!"

The People had only one primary word for both emotional and physical pain: *"kachinyehno."* In fact, with most languages, emotional pain is expressed with words that connote physical pain. For instance, "That was a real blow to his ego." "I'm scared to death!" "Those cutting remarks really hurt." "They really get in your face!" "I'm crushed!" "It's tearing me apart!"

It is no accident that language reflects the close relationship between physical and emotional pain, for all emotional pain impacts our bodies.

Imagine you have invested heart and soul in a painting. But when you display it, people are obviously unimpressed. Some are outright critical. Now, you may tell yourself that that's very disappointing. But to be honest, you would probably have to say that such a disappointment hurts you emotionally.

But why does such rejection hurt? Why do we say that something as unseen as rejection or fear causes us discomfort? Why do human languages imply that emotional pain hurts us physically? There are two reasons. The first is that disappointment or emotional pain of any kind is stressful. In turn, any kind of stress, no matter how slight, takes a toll on the body. Stress is what ages us and contributes to disease. Thus, even when we face a modest disappointment such as a rejected painting, it touches the physical side of our being. Added together over a lifetime, disappointment and emotional pain hurt us a great deal. The proverbial "Sticks and stones may break my bones, but words can never harm me" is simply not true.

The second reason emotional pain hurts us physically is that it triggers responses in our lower brain using nerve tracts that also convey physical pain. The lower brain in turn plays a primary role in our emotions. This explains in part why depression and anxiety can increase physical pain, and physical pain increases depression and anxiety.

There is never any emotional pain without some amount of physical stress, and there is no physical pain that does not touch our emotions. As we shall see, our response to physical pain and emotional pain can even be interchangeable.

So interwoven are emotional and physical pain, we can use one to mask the other. For instance, when we are feeling angry we may lose awareness of a minor toothache. In contrast, when we experience a major toothache we may not have the energy to get angry.

Our Need for Pain

It is natural to protest the presence of physical and emotional pain. We sometimes attempt to control one with the other. We don't like bumps, bruises, itches, and aches any more than we do fear, rejection, loneliness, and grief. Pain can be tough to live with. But it would be far harder to live without it. As much as we may protest pain, we need it if we are to stay emotionally and physically healthy. Our need for physical pain can be demonstrated by looking at Hansen's disease (leprosy). Hansen's disease damages those nerves which send pain messages to the brain.

We have probably all seen pictures of bodies disfigured by Hansen's disease. Hands or fingers and sometimes feet are gone, and facial tissue is badly scarred. Contrary to what was thought in ancient times, the disease does not eat away the person's flesh. Instead, it slowly destroys the person's body by preventing pain signals from reaching the brain to warn the person that injury has occurred to the body.

People normally use pain to unconsciously determine physical limits. We adjust hand pressure against a faulty door handle. It resists us so we readjust pressure carefully across our hand and turn harder. It won't move. Finally we grab a tool to force the door open, or we allow some penetrating oil to seep in, and we try later. But a person with Hansen's disease may apply enormous pressure on the first try and move the handle without feeling the damage being done to his hand. It becomes a war of flesh versus steel. Since no pain occurs, the tissue of his hand is destroyed day after day until his hands are deformed and can no longer function. Of course this trauma not only affects the person physically, but emotionally.

"There is never any emotional pain without some amount of physical stress, and there is no physical pain that does not touch our emotions."

The person with Hansen's disease fails to adjust for physical pain in part because he denies that he is being damaged. Although it is obvious the person doesn't like to watch himself deteriorate any more than we would, he allows himself to anyway. In daily routines he wounds his feet, hands, and fingers until their mechanical structures fail. Sores go unattended, and tired muscles and damaged tendons are stressed mercilessly.

We might be tempted to think, *Why doesn't the person simply use extreme caution and thereby prevent physical damage from occurring at all?* First, he cannot be careful enough to cover every contingency. Everything in the world around him is potentially destructive in ways those with a protective nervous system would never imagine.

Second, and probably more important, he is driven by emotional pain. A child with Hansen's disease, for instance, may try to run and keep up with other kids, even when he knows his ankles are damaged and need healing.

People with Hansen's disease push their limits as do others. They still feel and avoid emotional pain, perhaps more than most people. They need to cope with emotional pain as certainly as they do the absence of physical pain.

Emotional pain is an important indicator to everyone. When we push away emotional pain, deny or medicate it, we are in reality pushing away important warning signs of stress. To "think away" or medicate emotional pain is to place yourself in the same jeopardy as the person with Hansen's disease turning the faulty doorknob. A war is created between our willpower and the "steel" of reality.

Of course, all of us routinely disregard some minor physical and emotional pain, such as when we meld ourselves to a hard seat because we want to see the end of a long ball game, or when we continue working even though we have a headache, or when we strain to lift heavy weights in a workout. Similarly, we may choose to ignore an occasional rejection or insult that brings us emotional pain. Overcoming incidental and minor pain is a daily routine. However, if we routinely ignore too much emotional and physical pain, or any pain which warns us of peril, the outcome is sure to be destructive.

Pain may be bitter medicine, yet the destruction it prevents is far more distasteful. We need the constant influence of physical and emotional pain to keep us alive and healthy by keeping us in touch with our vulnerability.

The Mind-Body Connection

Have you ever stopped to think where fear, anger, and feelings of pleasure come from? Have you ever noticed that emotions can move you as much as you move them?

An often overlooked aspect of our being is the mind-body connection. Our bodies not only play a major role in shaping our emotions, but also in contributing to our experience of emotional pain.

Pain indicates the presence of emotional or physical stress just as clearly as the temperature gauge in a car indicates the presence of engine heat. Pain must be transmitted through nerve fibers and registered in our brains if we are to be aware of it.

We have both slow and fast nerve fibers. If you used an electrode to stimulate the fast fibers, a person would feel pressure sensations. In contrast, stimulus of the slow fibers could produce pressure or temperature sensations, but if the stimulus of the slow fibers increased, the result would be pain. Now if you stimulate slow and fast fibers at the same time, the pain would stop. Slow fiber activity seems to start pain while fast fiber activity can turn it off.

How our thinking and emotions influence our ability to use one type of nerve activity to block another painful one is something of a mystery. One clue, which we have already noted, lies in the fact that physical pain and emotions share some neural pathways.

How do we experience hurt physically? We touch or feel the physical world primarily through nerve endings located in our skin. Let's see how this occurs.

Pain messages begin at our skin and then travel to and through our brain via chains of nerve cells known as neurons. We have billions of neurons in complex circuits running throughout our nervous system. Information races from cell to cell as each cell in the circuit fires electrically. When each cell "fires" it causes the release of chemicals at the end of that cell in a microscopic space known as a synapse. These chemicals, called neurotransmitters, cause the next cell in line to fire just like the one before it.

Whether we are feeling pain, emotions, or just thinking, our nervous system uses electrochemical communication. When we think, for instance, chemical chain reactions are being repeated thousands of times a second as messages are sent throughout the brain.

Neurotransmitters are essential to both our logic and emotions as well as to our body functions. For instance, the kind and amount of neurotransmitters in our brain can either help us to think clearly or make us confused and mentally unstable. Within the mix of our brain's chemicals lies an essential ingredient of the mind-body connection. In fact, the same chemicals that mediate physical pain mediate emotional pain.

One transmitter causes pain even while touching our emotions. If we eat a hot jalapeño pepper, our nervous system automatically releases the transmitter P, which increases our sensation of pain. In turn, our system immediately releases other chemicals, such as endorphins and ACH (Acetylcholine), as pain blockers—sort of an internal fire extinguisher system. The gentle effect of endorphins may even motivate us to enjoy spicy chili or hot Cajun gumbo!

Some of the transmitters that help us cope with emotional and physical pain are held in reserve for life-threatening situations. You've probably heard stories of a desperate person single-handedly lifting the rear end of a car off a person pinned underneath. The massive release of deep reserve, stress-response neurochemicals makes this possible.

Depending on the part of the brain involved, our balance of neurotransmitters can cause our feelings to range from fearful and anxious to assertive and powerful. Some are capable of inducing pleasure or euphoria. Indeed, all of our emotions, behaviors, and moods are shaped in part by the chemicals in our brain. Other improper balances of transmitters contribute to such diseases as schizophrenia, obsessive-compulsive disorders, and many forms of depression. Individual balances of these brain chemicals are influenced by both environmental factors and genetics.

The right measure of neurochemicals helps us feel balanced, think clearly, and cope with both emotional and physical stress and pain.

Our delicate neurochemical system can easily be altered, exploited, or abused. In fact, illegal mind-altering drugs sold in black markets throughout the world have one thing in common: They change the balance of neurotransmitters in the brain, usually exploiting the neurotransmitter that naturally produces pleasure or masks pain.

Both doctors and drug addicts have learned to tinker with the body's pain relief system. For instance, addicts happily discover that recreational drugs cause the release of transmitters that prevent pain and provide pleasure. It looks like a free lunch. But later they discover such recreational drugs have depleted their natural supply of transmitters which buffer emotional pain. After getting high, and wasting their transmitters, addicts are worse off than ever. They feel both physically and emotionally sick. They lack the transmitters necessary to feel good emotionally. So what do they do? They use more drugs to feel better again, temporarily. It isn't just street addicts that play with neurochemicals. In later chapters we will look at how all of us manipulate our neurochemical system to influence our emotions.

Here is a sampling of neurotransmitters and the effect nervous system chemicals have on human behavior:

Endorphins (from the Greek words meaning "the morphine within") have essentially the same chemical makeup as morphine but are thirty times stronger. They function in our nervous system identically to morphine and produce the same painkilling and pleasurable effect. Endorphins are the hormones that function in the well-known runner's high. They even add to the experience of delight when you laugh or are excited, and they comfort you when you cry.

Norepinephrine (NE) and adrenaline production are triggered by stress and pain, with several profound effects. They raise the body's activity level and strength as well as increase mental concentration and assertiveness. When these are depleted or inadequate, the result is lethargy.

Serotonin (5-HT) is clearly linked to our ability to cope with emotional and physical pain. Excess serotonin produces euphoria; insufficient serotonin is associated with both depression and agitation.

Dopamine (DA) affects emotional moods, including those of well-being.

Acetylcholine (ACH), the most prevalent neurotransmitter in the body, plays a crucial role in harmonizing other transmitters. It is also involved in memory functions.

Beyond these dominant transmitters, numerous other brain chemicals affect the experience of well-being, stress, and emotional pain.

Masking Pain

Our neurochemical system can help us do amazing things.

One church sat on the edge of town, surrounded by chaparral and manzanita bushes. One day, wildfire rushed toward the south end of town, pushed out of the hills by a warm easterly wind. Firefighters from nearby communities were battling a major fire line south of town, so only two crewmen on a small truck could help the church protect its vulnerable wooden building from the advancing firestorm. At the edge of the parking lot one of the firefighters dripped fuel to start a backfire. It caught just in time and sped out to meet the incoming flames. The racing backfire left a wonderful stretch of blackened ground standing between the church and destruction.

As flying embers fell from the sky, Deacon Matteson scurried from one end of the roof to the other, smothering sparks. At least people thought it was Deacon Matteson. He had such bad arthritis that no one had ever seen him even walk fast, much less run.

Down on the lawn Deacon Keemle had stepped on an abandoned rake and badly punctured his right foot. He was hopping unceremoniously on the other.

Both these men were exhibiting natural responses to pain. Without realizing it, both were releasing extra norepinephrine, dopamines, and especially endorphins to cope with pain.

Their responses were both emotional and physical diversions—in reality, "backfires" that protected them against the "wildfire" of pain. They were fighting fire with fire!

Not only do we get ourselves excited when we are in pain, but emotional and physical pain make us excited. Look closely at Deacon Keemle dancing on one foot. His nervous system is definitely on the move.

Although uncomfortable in the long run, physical excitement is an effective short-term weapon against pain, especially incidental pain. Have you ever noticed how a toddler falls and cries even before he knows if he is hurt? His crying excites his nervous system, diverting his attention and releasing endorphins just in case he is about to feel pain. Soon his mother helps with more excitement and diversion. "Johnny, look at the butterfly!" Assuming there really is a butterfly and there is no serious injury, his crying quickly stops.

As Hippocrates, the Father of Medicine, observed over two thousand years ago, pain can't handle competition. What Hippocrates had noted was this: Pain can be masked. Physical pain from different sources in our body will be no greater than its greatest source.

The next time you accidentally close a car door on two adjoining fingers, do an experiment (assuming you have the presence of mind). Notice you can transfer the focus of pain from one finger to another, and that when the focus is on one finger, pain subsides in the other. Thus one source of pain diverts attention from another. This is one reason we tense our face muscles to compete with a hammer blow to our thumb. We excite our nervous system to compete with itself. Such excitement will compete with either physical pain from a physical injury or emotional pain from an emotional injury.

In theory we could solve many of our problems with both emotional and physical pain by getting excited or physically intense in order to mask them. But there is a catch. Intensity requires energy, which eventually causes fatigue. In time, those trans mitters we indulge through intensity and excitement become depleted, creating the same effect recreational drugs have on addicts. In turn, our ability to handle stress is slowly compromised.

Physical exhaustion leads to emotional exhaustion. As we tire, we become less careful, more impulsive, and make more mistakes. Have you ever been too sharp with someone just because you were tired? Have you ever noticed how a worn shoelace breaks just when you're desperate to be somewhere on time? You're pulling harder than usual. Almost everything in our life gets harder as we become more weary.

The dilemma is inescapable; we simply cannot mask all of our emotional pain by getting excited about it or expending energy.

Coping with Pain

All of our efforts to avoid physical pain are limited, just as is the case with emotional pain. There are some forms of pain we can avoid some of the time and some forms of pain we escape some of the time, but we can't evade all pain all of the time.

If pain does not find a way into our life at one point it simply finds another access. Not only is pain persistent, the timing of its intrusion is routinely bad. In fact, our sense of pain frequently increases just when we are most vulnerable. One reason pain seems to "grow" on us is because of a phenomenon known as hyperalgesia, from "hyper" (above) and "algesia" (pain).

How does sensitivity to pain multiply? When we suffer tissue damage to our bodies, sensitivity to pain in that area increases. Thus, if we have a cut finger, we may feel extra pain if we even slightly bump that injury or if we are emotionally down. In addition, increased sensitivity to either emotional or physical pain increases sensitivity to the other. The same principle applies to our emotions. When we are a little discouraged or under pressure and it is stormy outside or we are late, a car that won't start is of greater concern.

When everything is going wrong and we're feeling great pain, it is much harder to be a sensitive, loving Christian. We always think that "tomorrow" we will do better. But only God knows how much pain or rest tomorrow will bring.

As we have noted, our emotions are affected by far more than our values and intentions. They are shaped by specialized parts of our brain, driven by neurochemicals, and influenced by the circumstances of our lives.

As all of us know, the circumstances in our lives are sometimes more than we can handle. Graciously, God has given our bodies a unique chemical to help us survive when emotional and physical pain wear us down.

What is the neurochemical we most use in coping with emotional and physical pain? The endorphin. So important is this natural "morphine" in helping us cope that if we were to inject ourselves with a morphine antidote, we would find ourselves unable to handle the least bit of stress. We would break into tears over nothing.

Let's say you're going for a bike ride on hilly roads. You start pedaling slowly because you're a little stiff from not having exercised that day.

"As all of us know, the circumstances in our lives are sometimes more than we can handle. Graciously, God has given our bodies a unique chemical to help us survive when emotional and physical pain wear us down."

Within half of a mile you feel yourself loosening up, but the first imposing hill really challenges your endurance. By the time you reach the top, you're huffing and puffing and pedaling furiously to keep from losing speed. Your thighs burn from lactic acid. You're very conscious of the biting pain, and you are relieved that you have reached the first summit.

The hills continue. You have miles to go, but soon your experience of pain is altered. Your muscles still hurt, the hills are still tough, but somehow it does not matter as much. The transition is so smooth you didn't even notice when it occurred. What happened on the ride? The hard pull up the first big hill caused the release of powerful painkilling endorphins.

Endorphins are behind the gentle and pervasive "glow" that follows any workout. The same effect occurs for the players in a bruising game of football. In fact, many players may not even notice their scrapes and bruises until well after the game is over and they are soaking in a tub.

Everyone indulges in the gentle glow of endorphins. They are reflected in the tears on the face of the mourner, in the laughter of the joke teller, and in the ambiance of a songfest or sports arena. They are invoked by the exciting, high pressure salesperson or even a sportscaster. They are pursued by parachutists, auto racers, horror movie fans, gamblers, and even rock climbers who casually refer to themselves as "adrenaline junkies." Indeed, people can readily become addicted to the pursuit of internal biochemical highs.

Endorphins can even impact our spiritual lives. There are few experienced pastors of large churches who have not noticed what happens after a busy week of special evangelistic meetings. Night after night, families tighten their schedules and make it to church. There is a great deal of joy and excitement. But the following week the phone starts ringing in the pastor's office. More people than usual get sick. More conflict arises. Signs of stress start breaking out all over the congregation. Personal and family problems that could have been brushed over before, now became big issues.

What went wrong? It isn't that the meetings were bad. The truth is that even fun events and excitement are stressful. Even though parties and concerts are enjoyable, they can wear you out. Remember, all of our emotions, even joy, are driven in part by our bodies.

Early in the week church members had plenty of endorphins. Halfway through the week they were digging into their reserves. Later in the week they were running on empty. When people stress themselves day after day, they will deplete their neurochemicals.

Many Christians have struggled with the phenomenon of adrenaline or morphine depletion precisely when they have tried their hardest to serve God. They pour themselves into a particular ministry but eventually find themselves "burned out." Then they feel trapped or depressed. Sometimes they even think God no longer loves them. How wonderful it is that our faith rests not on feelings, but on God's faithfulness to us! Every Christian needs to know that we can walk with God when we're down, just as surely as we can when we're up. Indeed, God's

Spirit moves us, comforts and helps us, whether we have the glow of endorphins or not.

Christians need to be realistic about pain. God does not remove every physical limitation. Any Christian who overextends himself or herself on long and difficult projects (including ministry) should expect to feel the results. The "adrenaline blues," that slowed-down, "I can't get going" feeling, doesn't mean you lack faith. It just means you've overextended yourself. If you slow down for a while, the feeling will probably turn around.

Nothing of this world works perfectly: Adrenaline highs do not last forever and we cannot always live life on a dead run. Any diversion or protection from pain, be it physical or emotional, laughter or tears, is subject to failure, limits, and abuse. All chemical and emotional diversions from pain eventually deteriorate, and pain will compete for our attention once again.

There will be times when, as with Francine in the Amazon jungle, God will require more of you than you are able to give. But He will also help you. Those are the times to remember what the apostle Paul says about our position in Jesus: "For when I am weak, then I am strong" (2 Corinthians 12:10, NKJV).

Part 1: The Problem of Pain

TWO

COMING
TO TERMS
WITH PAIN

"Consider what God has done: Who can straighten what he has made crooked? When times are good, be happy; but when times are bad, consider: God has made the one as well as the other. Therefore, a man cannot discover anything about his future."

—Ecclesiastes 7:13

TWO

Coming to Terms with Pain

A young mother agonizes over her hospitalized toddler who just yesterday was bursting with activity and mischief. An unemployed man grimaces at the bank's notice that his house is scheduled for a sheriff's sale. A disfigured man comes out only in the shadow of night. A widow sits alone with her heartache. Pain is everywhere; it is inescapable; and it will touch all of our lives in some way.

I once took my three-year-old boy in for stitches. A tumble had left a nasty gash on the top of his head. After a laborious conversation en route to the hospital, I finally gave up trying to convince him that he needed to see the doctor. I wasn't about to negotiate with him, and he wasn't listening to me. It was not his first trip to the hospital.

I helped hold him down. The long needle repeatedly probed the inner edges of the wound where the lidocaine would be most effective. It was an unappreciated gift of healing from an emergency room doctor. It reminded me that God uses pain to bring about healing.

No philosophy, religion, or scientific system has the ability to dispense with pain. Neither our bodies nor our emotions will ever, in this life, escape pain's demands.

Inner and Outer Pain

In the long run physical pain is inescapable. We could live our lives in a germfree, plastic bubble and our bodies would still feel the sting of stress. Our attempts to insulate from emotional pain are equally futile, and there is a simple reason we can find no perfect hiding place. Emotional pain is as inescapable as physical pain. It not only flows from our external world, where we can scarcely avoid it, it also emerges from our inner being. We find ourselves trapped: If we turn outward, we experience emotional pain; if we turn inward, we will encounter pain as well.

31

Let's look at both experiences of pain. Outside pain is the most obvious and typically emerges in our social world. It is caused by such experiences as criticism, rejection, and general emotional stress. Financial problems, double binds, conflicts, pressure to produce, and fear are common sources of outside pain.

In contrast, inner pain is there whether we are experiencing obvious outside pain or not. We all experience inner pain from our awareness of current failures as well as from the emotional scar tissue of yesterday's fears and vulnerabilities. Such pain often reflects our deepest emotional identity, shaped by our many emotional battles, some long since fought but never really finished.

Inner and outer emotional pain mask each other just as do physical and emotional pain. When we feel outer pain, we have less sense of inner pain. For instance, our busy life-styles often mask the inner pain that is a persistent, though at times shadowy, traveling companion. The opposite is also true. When we are not fighting to survive, we are more apt to feel the weight of our inner pain.

Inner pain should not be disregarded. I know a man who had everything: His house was paid for; he was happily married; he enjoyed a secure, fulfilling job; his son was a football captain with a university scholarship; and his daughter had been accepted into medical school. Everything seemed to be just right. Yet, after years of success, this man suddenly became disillusioned and sank into deep depression. Everyone wondered what happened to this high achiever. What had gone wrong? The man was caught by his long-avoided inner pain.

When we enjoy extended periods of prosperity and well-being we are quite vulnerable to the hidden dilemma of inner pain. It is all too easy to give our hearts to the pursuit of a carefree life. But then the inevitable happens. We discover there is a limit to what is new and exciting. One day we may be struck by the fact that time is quickly passing and that all we enjoy and value in this earthly life is on its way to oblivion. We acutely feel what Solomon concluded about life: "Everything is meaningless" (Ecclesiastes 1:2). Solomon's observation addresses the crisis we face when we become aware of how limited we are in changing the nature of life. Had he not trusted God, Solomon's penetrating insight may well have derailed him.

How limited are we? We never grow younger and we never live outside the physical and emotional boundaries God sets upon us. Glory is fleeting. The more we have of this world, the more we ultimately stand to lose. Each day lived is a day closer to death. Each day, the body is less able to do those things we once thought so important and enjoyable.

Our emotional scars, limitations, and life itself contribute to our sense of inner pain. Our limitations and failures are personalizations of what the apostle Paul calls the "groaning" of creation (Romans 8:22). We do not always pay attention to the hidden discomfort of inner pain. And though such pain is easy to disregard for a season, that does not prevent it from affecting us.

Just as outer emotional pain can either cause us to rebel against God or lead us to trust Him more, inner emotional pain can cause us to either rebel against God or turn to Him. When inner pain beckons, we can choose to ignore it or feel it. We can run from it or feel it, and so let it remind us of the fragility of life, the necessity of faith, and the hope of eternity.

It is easy to run from the pain caused by our limitations. We can see a dentist for a toothache; we can read advice columns addressing our daily problems; we may even imitate the way other people respond to outer painful experiences. But when pain comes from within, it is harder to know if we are responding in a healthy way.

When we habitually avoid or deny personal inner pain, we make it difficult for even friends to be aware of our struggles. As the years pass, however, the inner pain we have avoided may be growing into an active volcano. We can discreetly go on protecting ourselves from inner pain; unfortunately, if by chance it waits a long time to surface, there may be no one to warn us of the consequences.

One of the reasons we have so much trouble coming to terms with emotional pain is our persistent assumption that we can somehow fix it. But to eliminate emotional pain we would have to change creation itself, for, as noted earlier, all emotional pain is linked to physical pain.

So when we reject emotional pain, we are in effect rejecting all pain and thus running the risk of trying to circumvent the limits God has put upon humanity. In other words, when we accept emotional pain, we are far less likely to make the mistake of trying to recreate God's world.

Promises of Difficulty

We need to approach the problem of pain from the perspective of the God who is communicated in Scripture. We need to come to terms with a God who allows pain. "I am the Lord, and there is no other. I form the light and create darkness, I bring prosperity and create disaster; I, the Lord, do all these things" (Isaiah 45:6–7).

The Bible speaks to the dilemma pain presents. Listen to God address Adam after his rebellion in the garden of Eden:

"Cursed is the ground because of you; through painful toil you will eat of it all the days of your life. It will produce thorns and thistles for you, and you will eat the plants of the field. By the sweat of your brow you will eat your food until you return to the ground, since from it you were taken; for dust you are and to dust you will return" (Genesis 3:17–19).

These are tough words and certain promises. In them God warns us that when the sun rises, so will new difficulties. Each day will have its own rough edges. Life is as Jesus promised: "Each day has enough trouble of its own" (Matthew 6:34).

The pain Adam experienced was not just a matter of punishment. God chose pain to limit Adam. As pain entered the picture, Adam was obliged to feel the sharp edge of emotional and physical stress. He would age, and with the passage of time, die. Adam's descendants inherited the same promise of pain, for God destined it to be an inseparable companion in every earthly pilgrimage. Adam was obliged to learn to cope with pain, and so are we.

Perhaps at first Adam tried to banish from his mind the promise that he would return to dust. Perhaps he perceived death as a strange problem for tomorrow; after all, no one had died before. But pain was another matter. Pain could not be brushed aside. Soon, Adam experienced his first thistle punc ture, the first flesh torn from his toe, and his first headache, depression, and bout with anxiety.

Adam began facing the problem of restraint. He could no longer do whatever he wanted for as long as he wanted, in whatever way he wanted. As the seasons passed, the plight worsened. Each passing year his bones ached more, and his muscles responded less. Adam and Eve must have tried to console one another, and even to remove each other's pain. But their bodies continued to weaken, to become ill, and to age. They were dying.

The promise God gives us in Genesis 3 is more certain than taxes. It is the law of pain. We will face stress, and with that stress we will experience actual pain: from an aching joint to thorns in the heart—grief, anxiety, depression. It's impossible for us to live without stress and aging. It's likewise impossible to live without both emotional and physical pain. As with Adam, so for us there is always some form of "sweat," "weeds," or "thorns" to confound our progress on this earth.

Persistent trouble is not our only problem. God has said that we must die. Death is the ultimate result of the accumulation of stress in our lives. That stress will impact us as injury causing damage and disease or, conversely, as disease causing injury. Every one of us, barring the Lord's return, will inevitably sicken and die or be injured and die, all the while under God's compassionate care.

Many people hope they can go through life without ever getting seriously ill. Such a dream is, in a real sense, impossible because of death. All death, except that caused by specific injury, reflects system failure of some sort within the body; in other words, disease. Even death by natural causes is, in reality, death by degenerative disease. (Some doctors therefore refer to life as a fatal disease.) Logic dictates that each must wane slowly, sporadically, and sometimes painfully.

In short, God will not preserve us from deterioration. We will continue to get colds, headaches, and sprained ankles. Such physical stress is, in fact, part of our dying. But we fight it. Even our emotional pain is often like a bad case of the flu! We toss and turn to get a better position, but we can never find one that makes us quite comfortable. We fight it as well.

God may remove a given disease at His choosing, especially in response to our prayer. Even so, a new disease will come, deterioration will occur, and we will ultimately die. Even Lazarus had to die—a second time.

Growth through Pain

I recently talked with a man who was facing surgery for a chronic intestinal problem. He was busy trying to discover what Satan was doing in his life. "I'm believing God, but why shouldn't this problem get healed?" he complained.

"I would be surprised if God didn't permit such difficulties," I said. "Didn't He promise to do so when He confronted Adam in the Garden of Eden?" I asked.

Has God not promised us difficulty? We must be cautious about attributing all our problems to the devil. In fact, I often suggest to people that they should think twice before rejecting any given form of pain God directs their way. After all, if God wants us to grow through an experience of pain and we evade it, He may well send yet another painful trial—and it could be less preferable! Isn't it best to always accept our merciful Father's first choice of pain for our spiritual growth?

Late one night I heard two grinding crashes on the road in front of our house. On this foggy evening a large oak had fallen across the road. Seconds later a car smashed into it, carrying the tree trunk about twenty feet up the road. I phoned for help and raced outside. The driver of the car was a Christian friend I had known for years. He had suffered some lacerations and had broken an arm against the steering wheel.

We talked again the next morning by phone. He knew God had sent Christian friends when he needed help, and he was exceedingly grateful for that. He was safe, and he was grateful for that. Yet he just couldn't understand what spiritual force had wrecked his car. Who had let the tree fall? He couldn't imagine that God may have allowed this accident as one of many possible trials. Let's look at what the Scripture says:

"Dear friends, do not be surprised at the painful trial you are suffering, as though something strange were happening to you. But rejoice that you participate in the sufferings of Christ" (1 Peter 4:12–13).

"The Lord said to him [Moses], 'Who gave man his mouth?

Who makes him deaf or mute? Who gives him sight or makes him blind? Is it not I, the Lord?'" (Exodus 4:11).

Listen to Job respond to his critic Bildad: "Though I cry, 'I've been wronged!' I get no response; though I call for help, there is no justice. He has blocked my way so I cannot pass" (Job 19:7–8).

We know from the story of Job and from Scripture in general that God had a profound purpose in the trials He permitted to touch His servant Job. From the depths of Job's mortality and grief came victory. This is a rich metaphor of the gospel story of Jesus' death and resurrection—the very image of the Messiah who would one day take Job's suffering upon himself. It was Job who in his pain was pressed to declare:

"Oh, that my words were recorded, that they were written on a scroll, that they were inscribed with an iron tool on lead, or engraved in rock forever! I know that my Redeemer lives, and that in the end he will stand upon the earth. And after my skin has been destroyed, yet in my flesh I will see God; I myself will see him with my own eyes" (Job 19:23–27).

Placing Our Trust in God

While we may agree that trusting God is important, actually doing so can be quite difficult. When we hurt, we often wonder if God still loves us. Is He really aware of our suffering? Do we need to pray harder or longer to let Him know we need Him? Of course He knows.

Our trust of God does not grow in a vacuum. Just as we trust friends on the basis of time spent with them, so we learn to trust God on the basis of time spent with Him. For our trust to grow, we must experience emotional pain, and then experience God's help. When it comes to faith, both emotional and physical pain force us to determine our source of strength. When the Good Shepherd leads us through painful valleys either we will hold more tightly to His hand or we will run from Him, desperately seeking our own security.

Some of the richest times in my relationship with God have come during the toughest times in my life. Those have been the times God has taught me to depend on Him.

Once, when our band was traveling cross-country on a prison ministry tour, we had to drive from the West Coast to

Tennessee on a very tight schedule. We spent the first night and day broken down in the California desert, greasy and sweating, trying to repair our vehicles. Finally, we were able to drive our vehicles toward the California border town of Needles. By now it was about nine at night. We were excited, for we were going to get out of California within twenty-four hours after all!

I still remember the call on the C.B. from the tail van.

"Breaker Red Bird, you're not going to believe this," sighed Pete, the driver of the blue service van.

"Go Blue, this is Red," I said. "What's the problem?"

"I hear a rod noise in the engine."

"That can't be!" I shouted into the C.B. "That's a new engine! Are you sure?"

"You'd better listen to it, Steve. I'm pulling over now. Blue out."

The rod was knocking badly, and the van's oil pressure was dropping. *Well, that does it,* I thought. *This trip is finished. At any moment that rod is going to go through the side of the block. That engine needs to be shut down now so there will be something to save.*

We limped into Needles and parked in a vacant lot. About midnight we gathered in a circle to pray. "What do you want us to do, Lord?" we prayed. "How shall we deal with this crisis?" I will never forget the answer God gave each of us simultaneously, *I never told you to stop!*

At first we were astonished, but the encouragement of the Lord was so strong it could not be ignored. Immediately, everyone reloaded and we drove nonstop to Tennessee, where a rebuilt engine block was waiting for us (God didn't tell us to come back on the bad engine). But even if our trip had stopped, that would have been fine. God would have had something to teach us even in that event.

When the believer encounters difficulty, he needs to accept it and press on as God enables. As believers, we can have confidence, for Christ states, "In this world you will have trouble. But take heart! I have overcome the world" (John 16:33). We should trust God even when we cannot foresee anything good resulting from our pain and circumstances. Our problems do not elude God's surveillance. It is never an accident when He allows trouble to come our way.

What we believe about the place of pain in our lives determines how we cope with it. If we believe that pain belongs in our lives because God has ordained it, then we will be more inclined to accept it. When stress and pain enter our lives we must choose to either resist or leave our situation in God's hands. It is very difficult to live both ways—to trust God with our pain and try to control it at the same time.

When I was training for my pilot's license, I learned a valuable lesson. As my instructor and I cruised along at five thousand feet, I donned a hood to obstruct my vision out the cockpit window. I could no longer use the horizon to determine the plane's actual position. My instructor had me close my eyes. After placing the plane in an awkward position, he told me, "Open your eyes. It's your plane." I could look only at the instruments to correct the plane's attitude. After scanning the gauges, I had seconds to respond to what the control panel displayed. The seat of my pants said I was in one position, but the instruments said I was in another. I knew I had to trust the instruments. Every pilot is taught to believe the instruments or face certain disaster.

When we experience pain, the tendency is to fly our lives by instinct, by the seat of our pants, not by the instruments. We want to control the painful situation. But Scripture trains us to trust God! During difficult times we must remember that God is in control of our pain. We must remember that God loves us and has our best interest in mind. We must remember to respond to pain the way He tells us, not on the basis of how we feel.

If we leave our pain in God's hands—trusting Him implicitly with both the pain and joy of our lives—we are in for a sure adventure, safe flight, and good landing. God's counsel will always be right.

Maintaining a healthy outlook on the difficult situations in life is a matter of accepting life on God's terms. Indeed, it is a matter of accepting our pain on God's terms.

THREE

EMBRACING PAIN

"The Lord is close to the brokenhearted and saves those who are crushed in spirit."

—Psalm 34:18

THREE

Embracing Pain

Deep in their hearts, some Christians believe that faith in God will serve as a protection against pain. They hope that serious trouble or tragedy will somehow bypass them simply because they believe in God. The assumption, for instance, that financial prosperity is the normal life-style for all believers only feeds denial about how hard life really is for most Christians around the world.

The Scripture demonstrates that life, even for the best Christians, will not necessarily be easy. We know that some of Jesus' disciples struggled through life, some facing terrible deaths. We are in the same position. God may allow us to live in suffering or rejoice in peace, for the control of pain is not in our dominion.

We know that God allows His sunshine and rain to benefit the unrighteous as well as the righteous. But the inverse is also true: He allows great pain to afflict the righteous as well as the unrighteous. As Christians we should not assume that we ought to have it easy while non-Christians have it hard. In fact, if we do run from emotional pain on the assumption that a hard life is not meant for us, we may be denying exactly what God has chosen for challenging our faith! How tragic if we spend our lives running, not understanding that the pain we must really fear is pain that is outside of God's will.

God always has a purpose in the pain we so routinely resist, even if that purpose is hard for us to see. "Indeed as the sufferings of Christ overflow to us, so, through Christ, does our consolation overflow. When we are made to suffer, it is for your consolation and salvation" (2 Corinthians 1:5–6, *Jerusalem Bible*).

Denying Emotional Pain

There are times when denial of emotional pain actually helps us survive stress. Consider the child who mentally blocks out an abusive relationship in order to cope with life. As adults, all of us block out some emotional pain, since there is no way we can face every problem at once.

Unfortunately, denial can be abused. If we can deny a little, why not deny a lot! And how do we know what is healthy to deny? Even if we strive to be honest, it can be very hard to know when to deny our problems and when to face them. Indeed, breaking out of denial is like escaping from a mine that is caving in. We may know we have to get out, but it's too dark to see where we're going. It is only God who can best show us how and when to accept emotional pain.

Like it or not, denial can be a real problem for Christians, especially in the area of ministry. As with the Pharisee and the scribe in the Parable of the Good Samaritan, it is all too easy for us to look away from suffering in the world around us. It is also quite possible to get out of balance and become an unhealthy Good Samaritan. We can be so involved in doing ministry that we lose touch with our own emotional needs and limits.

Although we should never hesitate to pour ourselves out in God's service, we should not, in the process, run from the emotional pain God allows in our lives.

Have you ever put off a responsibility or created a flimsy excuse? Everyone indulges in a little denial. For instance, whenever we overeat, or try not to think about an unpleasant event, or even when we read a challenging Scripture but think it applies to someone else, denial is at work.

High pressure salespeople find our episodic denial especially useful. Have you ever been talked into a purchase while being steered away from a glaring flaw in the deal? Only later do you realize that had you really looked at the facts, your money would still be in your pocket!

I had this conversation once with an inmate: "Yeah, I think drug and alcohol counseling is great for people who need it," the inmate told me. "I wish I could get my girlfriend to talk to you. She has a serious drinking problem."

Our entire conversation focused on her drinking until I changed the subject.

"So how long before you're out of here?" I asked.

"One more year," he said. "I've had real bad luck. I've been busted four times for drunk driving."

Bad luck? This inmate had no idea he had his own problem with alcohol. He was in a condition known as denial—the tendency to ignore problems and disown the truth.

Denial is a subtle and often clever escape from emotional pain. It is how we deal with the reality that our world is not what we want it to be. It is a tool we use to cloud the past and find refuge in the present.

Denial is one of the biggest problems any person faces: denial of personal pain, denial of a destructive problem, denial of one's own vulnerability.

While we all use denial to cope with emotional pain, we never do so without risk. Denial catches up with anyone who has ignored a persistent problem, failed to accept his or her limitations, or sidestepped the truth.

In the beginning, denial can be modest. But since denial often grows when it is unchallenged, it may only be a matter of time until it becomes too great to overcome.

Denial can be quite dangerous. Overeaters, alcoholics, and addicts, for example, often deny their addictions at great personal cost. I know one gentleman who, in the early stages of alcoholism, left a garden party where he had indulged in a few too many. Around the corner, still within earshot, his car careened off the road. No one was hurt, but he had flattened a fence and totaled his vehicle. Walking back to the garden party (just ahead of the police) he addressed his "bad luck" with classic denial. "I hit a slick spot on the road and dented my car." With the truth clouded by denial, not even an expensive accident and jail time would stop this alcoholic on his personal road to disaster.

It is not until we face the cold facts about what is and is not healthy in our lives that change and growth are likely to occur. It is sometimes difficult to admit our own denial, however; for when we are in emotional pain, facing denial may be the very last thing we want to consider.

Active Denial

One way to cope with emotional pain is with active denial. That occurs when we intentionally force emotional pain from our minds. Sometimes we can work wonders with it!

I once talked to a woman who was deeply involved in a cult

that denies the existence of evil. She was committed to seeing life in positive terms. What an experience it was to visit her home. There, nothing was ever wrong. She even saw the tragic headlines on the newspaper resting on the coffee table as an illusion. Crossing the room, she would sweep open the drapes with a flourish, saying, "Oh, what a glorious day!" Several deep breaths later she was still elaborating on the splendor of that day. I grew less convinced with each statement; the weather wasn't that good. How distant she seemed. How astounding that she could deny so much!

Few people can maintain such blatant denial in every area of their lives. Instead, most of us use active denial only as a convenience, changing our perception of the world whenever it best serves our purpose. All of us have some active denial. For instance, if we cannot face the fact that tens of thousands of children starve to death each day, we just don't think about it. We may even develop a handy argument as to why we can do nothing to help. In time, we may not think about such starvation at all.

Passive Denial

Another way to cope with emotional pain is with passive denial. People often think all denial is a matter of believing something that is untrue. Not exactly. Most denial is the unintentional failure to deal with pain.

Addicted people routinely get lost in passive denial. For instance, as a counselor, I hear alcoholics talk quite candidly about their drinking problems and the serious havoc alcohol is wreaking on their lives. They do not appear to be denying their problem at all. Nevertheless, these alcoholics continue to drink themselves to death. They really don't want to die, nor do they intend to. They talk about the real world without ever dealing with it.

This is passive denial. It is subtle, easier, and just as common as active denial. Whenever we practice passive denial, we do not set out to change reality. We either ignore it or simply put off dealing with it until tomorrow.

One recovering heroin addict talked about her heavy habit of passive denial. While driving, she occasionally changed lanes even though she could not clearly see the traffic behind her.

Since she was already under tremendous stress, she didn't want to be bothered straining to look back. *Maybe,* she thought, *nothing will be there.* Ignoring potential disaster, she just cringed and changed lanes, awaiting a potential scrape or horn blast.

Denial is especially dangerous for drug addicts. Even though they know better, weary addicts in "shooting galleries" will disregard the dirt and encrusted blood on a needle in their rush to obtain the relief contained in the syringe.

Denying Sickness and Disease

Miracles and healing are an important part of the Christian response to emotional and physical pain. But even here Christians can become caught up in denial. It is all too easy to avoid the hard truth about disease and mental anguish.

I once visited a group of believers who had gathered for an evening service. They were gracious, compassionate people. At the close of the worship time most of the participants gathered to pray for a young woman who was afflicted with severe cerebral palsy. They gently helped her to the center of the room, made a circle around her, and prayed. She desperately wanted healing. They desperately wanted to see her healed.

The group prayed earnestly with an assumption that is common to many believers: God wants, in all circumstances, to remove sickness, pain, and suffering from our lives. When they had finished their fervent prayer, believing that God would heal, they gathered at the opposite end of the room to socialize. The girl, still not healed, wept.

The others didn't approach her to offer comfort not because they didn't care, but rather because they feared it would show a lack of faith. They instinctively declined talking to the sick girl who, according to their belief system, should have been well—not crying! In truth, they were denying the girl's disease.

The denial in the room was quite varied. Some just ignored the dilemma. Some questioned the girl's faith rather than their own. Others held the belief that the healing might take place later that night, or was happening so gradually that no one could see it. Every explanation was covered except that the girl was simply not healed.

Perhaps all of us have been in the position of not knowing

how to help those in pain. Sometimes we wonder why we weren't helped ourselves. How often have we asked, Since God can do all things, why doesn't He relieve my pain? We can easily fall into the subtle trap of Christianized positive thinking. We want things to be different and assume that if we pray and expect the preferred result, it will occur. That's precisely when denial starts and our credibility is drawn into question.

Denial related to healing can be terribly blatant. A woman once told me how she had just been healed from a cold. As we spoke, a sturdy cough escaped her mouth. She quickly told me she was "rebuking" the cold.

A man on crutches routinely ate breakfast in a restaurant where a friend and I occasionally stopped. My friend quietly shared his faith with the man. In response, the man displayed his bitterness toward Christians. He related how a woman who worked in his office had kept telling him that if he became a Christian, God would heal his legs. Now the man was in denial, doubting that God or anyone still loved him. In turn, the woman who had so disturbed him was also in denial about the sovereignty of God and His authority to do exactly as He chose with the man's legs.

If we believe God does not want us or those around us to live in a world of suffering and pain, we must deny the world around us or, worse yet, unintentionally cause other people to suffer more through false hope.

I know of one woman who prayed for a friend and assured her the lump in her breast was cured. From then on the friend refused all treatment. The lump was a growing cancer which finally took her life. Everyone in their small town watched the terrible tragedy unfold. In addition to the unnecessary loss of a life, the devout woman who proclaimed the healing was devastated and became a recluse.

At the heart of this tragedy was not a lack of God's mercy; rather, it was the failure to understand why and when God heals. It was the denial of the reality of disease and pain.

I received a call from a Christian leader whose small child was diagnosed as having brain cancer. The man was distraught over his child's disease, the mounting medical bills, and the challenge of caring for the child.

He told me how everyone was claiming that the child was

going to be healed. Special prayer vigils and fasts had been called on the boy's behalf.

"I'm not sure how to pray," he said.

I replied, "Let me ask you a very hard question. What do you think God wants to do in this situation?"

He paused. "I think he wants to take the boy home."

We prayed together on the phone that God would stand with him during this ordeal. Following the prayer, he said it was the first time he had felt peace and relief since the boy fell ill.

Two months later the boy died.

Denial can be a tough habit to break, and being honest about how the world really is does not necessarily make life easier. In fact, it can make it much harder, for when we look at life the way it really is, our denial must decrease. When this happens, the emotional pain we feel may well increase. The good news is that when we accept such emotional pain, our faith is sure to grow!

Following God's Plan of Pain

We have discussed denial and failed presumptions about healing. "But doesn't the Bible teach us that God heals?" people ask. "We surely don't want to deny that! Doesn't it challenge us to have faith?" Of course God heals. As Christians we know that firsthand. And of course we must have faith. But exercising faith means depending on God and following His plan for our lives, not giving Him orders. The accounts of healing in the Bible and Jesus' discourses on faith clearly show that faith is a matter of understanding who God is, that He is in charge, and that He can do as He wishes. They do not support the idea that He must do what we want when we want Him to do it.

God heals according to His purpose. I have seen God's mercy miraculously heal a man in a hospital bed—a man who never acknowledged God in his life and had no intentions of doing so. Down the hall a Christian family who had lived sacrificially and loved God deeply did not see the healing of a child for whom they had prayed for months. Instead their young son died.

Was God unfaithful to the Christian family? Not at all. God promised them eternal life and the assurance that He would never leave them. That is all that family really needed at that time.

As much as we may like to deny pain and death, they are crucial. They are necessary rough spots in the road to eternal life. Despite our aversion to the unpleasant, pain and death help us to know God. Facing pain can help us ask real questions about faith: Why does God let us hurt? How can life be so unfair?

Once I attempted to comfort an elderly man during the last months of his life. This fine, respected servant of God had loved, served, and witnessed throughout his days. Now he was dying of cancer. He was brave, but he was also scared. He was surrounded by friends and he knew God was with him, yet he felt alone. Despite medication, his pain was excruciating. He cried out to have his life taken. In the final weeks, his tormented mind lashed out deliriously at imagined foes who mistreated him.

It was unusually quiet at this man's funeral. We worshiped, sang, and thanked God for his life. We were challenged by the Scriptures. Many people in the congregation felt quite peaceful, in part because they had not been touched by his suffering. But those of us who had been at his bedside were still rattled by his pain; it had touched our own hearts. No amount of denial could prevent the hard questions. How resilient was our own faith, and when might we ourselves enter such a valley?

My purpose is not to pursue a dark and pessimistic view of human existence. Rather, it is to help us be honest about the pain God has allowed in our lives. If we are not realistic about our pain, our solutions to it will be unhealthy. Faith will become a spiritual Disneyland, a place we visit for excitement and pleasure while keeping the first aid station, the labor, and the machinery concealed behind pretty fences and rich shrubbery.

We should remember that many times God does not explain why He brings either difficulty or times of ease. We should not try to analyze every source or incident of pain in our lives. Rather, we should follow the example of the prophet Job and accept as best we can what God chooses for us, be that joy or pain. If we take happiness from God's hand, must we not take sorrow too? (See Job 2:10.)

The enemy wants us to respond improperly to pain. As in the temptation of Jesus in the wilderness, Satan tries to tempt us with God's deliverance. The enemy wants us to stray from our primary call of servanthood—to give our lives away and to die for Christ's sake—in the name of finding deliverance, comfort, and security.

God does care for us. He is our deliverer. But as Oswald Chambers has observed: God is more concerned with our character than He is our comfort.

The words of an old Swedish hymn profoundly portray our Father's persistent care for us.

Day by day and with each passing moment,
Strength I find to meet my trials here;
Trusting in my Father's wise bestowment
I've no cause for worry or for fear.

Ev'ry day the Lord himself is near me
With a special mercy for each hour;
All my cares He fain would bear and cheer me;
He whose name is Counsellor and Pow'r.

The protection of His child and treasure
Is a charge that on himself He laid.
"As your days, your strength shall be in measure,"
This the pledge to me He made.

Help me, Lord, when toil and trouble meeting,
E'er to take as from a father's hand,
One by one, the days, the moments fleeting,
Till I reach the promised land.

God assures us, "See, I have engraved you on the palms of my hands" (Isaiah 49:16). Knowing this, we can trust our lives to our caring Father. God, who measures the duration and intensity of our pain, also ministers comfort to us in times of distress. But to experience His comfort, we must embrace our pain.

FOUR

DIVERSIONS
FROM PAIN

"It is for freedom that Christ has set us free.
Stand firm, then, and do not let yourselves be
burdened again by a yoke of slavery."

—Galatians 5:1

FOUR

Diversions from Pain

Denial is not the only avoidance pattern we have with pain. Whenever we become sick, undergo some great emotional distress, or experience some other form of suffering, we have the most human of reactions. We attempt to simply avoid it. Since we don't like to hurt, we strive to outmaneuver pain and stress. We take aspirin, look for comfortable places to sit, stay away from threatening situations, try not to get too cold or too hot, and, in general, design our lives to minimize our experience of stress and pain.

We instinctively slow down when we pass a police car, even if we're driving under the speed limit. We avoid the guy ahead of us in line who's raging like a maniac. We plan an evening so we won't be alone—or, on occasion, so we will be. We delicately avoid handling a cactus plant by its leaves. We mentally brace ourselves when we open our latest credit card bill.

Throughout life we learn to anticipate the onset of difficulty, stress, and emotional pain.

Nevertheless, our tendency to anticipate and avoid pain is so routine and subtle that we may be quite unaware that we do it at all. In part, this is because God designed our minds and bodies to automatically overcome stress and physical pain. Even hunger, thirst, and our other physical needs automatically cause internal imbalances and feelings of discomfort that motivate us to pursue relief. Our minds and bodies will avoid pain whether we think about avoiding it or not.

Our physical survival depends upon our healthy response to stress in the natural world. Such stress is often experienced as physical and emotional pain. Thus, our physical survival is based in part upon a natural law of pain. Simply put, pain is in the background of all behavior. It is an integral part of life, and if we are to be healthy, we must respond to pain in a healthy way.

If we don't avoid pain we can be seriously damaged. If we

avoid pain too much, that can hurt us too, as we develop any number of negative behavior patterns.

Then where can our natural avoidance of pain lead us? Anxiety, depression, anger, codependency, and compulsive behavior all follow in the wake of our very human tendency to overly avoid pain.

Mental Diversions

As we have noted, when emotional pain comes our way, we tend to emotionally "look away." In the most routine activities of daily living we find countless ways to avoid or divert our attention. It is a skill we develop from childhood. "Just think about something else for a while and stay busy," we are encouraged.

Why is diversion so important to us? Although pain is necessary for our survival, we do not like it. So we use mental activity to help us cope with stress and pain. Mental activity is quite useful in temporarily holding our attention and thereby masking our emotional pain. So when we are awake—and if we have the energy—we usually have something on our minds. We rarely sit still with our minds blank just for the fun of it. For instance, it is not likely that people will go to bed three hours early just so they can lie there and feel their emotions. It simply is not comfortable to ponder our emotional and physical stress-response system at work. Instead, we like to keep active on some level until we are able to sleep. Indeed we fill our days with diversion.

That is not to say all diversion is bad. Just as some avoidance of pain has its place, some diversion is also necessary. We need frequent breaks from the demands of life. How do we take breaks? We may daydream, read a book, play golf, repair a broken lamp, eat, head for the nearest mall, get into our work, reach for a goal, call a friend, or watch television. We may pursue very large diversions such as building a dream house or very small ones such as enjoying a quick cold drink. Almost anything will do.

I remember preparing for finals in my early college years. The noise of the dormitory was too great a distraction from studying for a difficult test. Unable to study in my dormitory, I decided to retreat to a small study booth in the library where I was certain nothing could distract me. Unfortunately, I took my fatigue and need for diversion with me. *That's an interesting pattern on the formica desk top,* I mused. *Where did that design come from?* Whispers from the next row penetrated my thinking. "Did you hear what Shelly did on her midterms in Barnett's U.S. history class?" Soon a noisy fly ventured near the seductive web of a spider. *Should I try to save the fly?* Everything seemed to distract me from my study.

Diversions—we are surrounded by them, and we create them. They help us not only avoid pain, they may even give us pleasure. Since we like pleasure, we usually choose the most exciting diversion possible. As long as we are avoiding pain, we will try to make the most of it.

Diversion is everywhere. Listen, for example, to conversations in operating rooms of major hospitals. "Sponge, retractor. Hey, doctor, who do you think is going to win the World Series? I don't think the Giants have a chance of getting there. I'm counting on the Dodgers."

"I don't think either one of them will make it," the doctor replies. "Scalpel, sponge. . . . I just hope a local team makes the playoffs."

Surgeons in the routine of the most spectacular heart surgery often talk about personal issues or even listen intently to a ball game while stitching and cutting. Any job can set the stage for diversion.

Highs and Lows as Diversion

"Highs" are another form of diversion. And it doesn't take a drug trip to experience a high. Everyone participates. A good book or movie will do. Suppose you watch a movie that is particularly boring. Your attention might be turned to the tingle of salty popcorn in your mouth, the semisoft gum stuck under the armrest, and the people talking about another movie one row over. They are diverting their attention too.

Compare those experiences with attending an exciting movie where your eyes are riveted to the screen and you lose all track of time. Half an hour after you leave the theater, you're still pondering the plot. That diversion has been a high, in part because it has diminished your awareness of stress and pain for a time.

Under the right circumstances a "low" can provide diversion much like a high. We can divert from pain and blunt its effect by becoming low—that is, by slowing down so that we might feel as little as possible. Overorganizing and structuring daily activities are similar means of trying to control pain. Some people, who operate on lows, create rigid schedules or patterns for getting through the day; nothing must ever threaten their personal routine. Such overcontrolling is used not only as a protection against stress but as a diversion from pain. Withdrawal, inactivity, denial, and repression are common ways of maintaining a low in order to control how much we feel. Consider the person who never does anything new, refusing to take chances or allow himself to experience deep feelings.

Some people never want to come down, and some people don't want to go up. Why? Because both changes could lessen the effect of their diversions. Some people stay too busy to experience their feelings and some people stay slowed down to better control what they feel. But in time, any high or low pays decreased dividends—and, in the end, avoided pain will always return.

When any experience providing an emotional high works well as an escape from pain, we tend to increase or sustain that high. And when a low works as an escape from pain, we tend to sustain that low. This begins the addictive pattern of pain avoidance.

Diversions: Temporary Relief

Unfortunately, people are rarely satisfied whether they are high or low or even in-between. It is difficult to value emotional pain, to understand Solomon's counsel that "sorrow is better than laughter" (Ecclesiastes 7:3). A person usually wants his world to be free from pain and the struggle that goes with it. Nevertheless, pain will inevitably be encountered. So when the law of pain gets our attention, we cope with it—but often in unhealthy ways.

Mike suffered bouts of depression. One day a car ran a red light and smashed into his motorcycle. He survived, but he had some permanent damage to his left arm. An out-of-court settlement dropped thirty thousand dollars into his pocket. He picked up the money late one afternoon. All his problems suddenly seemed to vanish. On the way home he stopped at a local car dealer. Unable to resist the new paint and naugahyde, Mike bought a car on impulse. His entire settlement was gone. It was a nice car, but soon the excitement dwindled and buyer's remorse settled in. There was another car he wanted more, but he had no money left. Depression quickly rolled back into Mike's life.

We can buy "breathers" from the feelings we don't want to experience, but the results of diversion are always temporary because the law of pain is permanent. In fact, our ability to use any diversion varies from day to day and moment to moment, depending upon how much energy we may have at the time and the effectiveness of the diversion.

At times we may link several individual diversions together for greater effect. As a general rule, the more dramatic the diversion, the more it distances us from pain. For example, the more entertainment, decorations, and food at a party, the more excitement there will be and the more that party will serve as a diversion from everyday problems. The general rules of diversion are "the more the merrier," "the bigger, the better," and "two are better than one."

Diversion is not a perfect solution for our emotional pain. Although it is quite natural for us to avoid stress, it is also natural to go one step further and try to divert attention from pain too often, if not altogether. Diverting too much or too often can place us on a collision course with the pain itself. We cannot escape the routine role of pain in our lives and pay no consequences.

Diversions, like daydreams, provide us with temporary relief; they rarely solve real problems. In fact, if the diversion takes the proportions of, say, a Hawaiian vacation on a credit card, significant payment is merely delayed.

There are times we must choose not to run, but rather to stop, feel, and listen. There are times to embrace the pain God allows in our lives.

FIVE

THE VALUE OF DEPRESSION

"Why are you downcast, O my soul? Why so disturbed within me? Put your hope in God, for I will yet praise him, my Savior and my God."

—Psalm 42:11

FIVE

The Value of Depression

"I don't want to live anymore!" Barbara cried. "Life is just too hopeless!"

Barbara had suffered bouts of depression since her early teens, but the attacks seemed to be getting worse.

"I just don't know what to do," she complained. "I hurt so bad inside."

"Barbara," I said, "I know it's been rough for a long time and you want some relief, but for now let's take some time to look at why you're hurting so much."

We talked for an hour, and after I referred Barbara for a physical examination to assess her depression for possible organic causes, she returned home. I had done what I could for her immediate emotional pain, but I knew the healing process would take time. Since there are no quick fixes for most cases of acute depression, Barbara would face yet another week of emotional struggle.

Understanding Depression

Depression is one of the toughest problems anyone can face. It afflicts countless people in all walks of life. Depression can take many forms. It can be mild, acute, short-lived, chronic, or seasonal. Depression can traumatize you, wear you out, or simply overwhelm you. It can be terribly hard to escape.

When most of us think of depression the first thing that may come to mind is, *Who needs it?* or *How can I escape it?* Sometimes I am asked, "Are Christians even supposed to get depressed?"

It is especially important that Christians understand depression. Too often, Christians are so committed to successful spiritual living that they ignore emotional limits. When these Christians finally recognize their depression, they are in such deep water it takes them a long time to swim to shore.

We have three basic options when faced with depression. We

can fight depression. We can give up and withdraw. Or we can accept depression and use it to our advantage. We will investigate the advantages of accepting depression. We will look at the helpful side of depression, what causes it, and even how to use it to our advantage.

With many physical problems, such as ulcers, diabetes, or allergies, knowing the cause is essential to the treatment. In the same way, understanding the causes and patterns of depression can help us soften its impact or even prevent it from occurring.

For many people depression is merely the result of running from emotional pain. For others, depression is a matter of having too much pain to handle. Sometimes depression is the result of a combination of these problems. Still other types are caused by organic disorders.

Gratefully, while there is no overnight cure for chronic or acute depression, most types do respond well to competent treatment. Indeed, much depression eventually improves whether treated or not. In most cases, however, depression is a long time in developing and a long time in receding.

Depression frequently results when chronic emotional pain traps us. Ironically, we are most likely to get trapped by depression when we are trying not to be depressed. Running from emotional pain is usually a mistake. We can indulge in denial or diversion. We can procrastinate, avoid, or simply try to control life's problems. But emotional pain can be relentless; there will be times when it catches us.

The Survival Instinct

The survival instinct for avoiding emotional pain can be as strong as the survival instinct for avoiding physical pain. Indeed, the will to survive shapes our behavior, our faith, and even our lives. It can also cause us trouble.

Many people avoid their emotions, only to get caught in compulsive behavior. Other people try just as hard to escape, only to be caught by depression.

But feelings of sadness, grief, and inner pain are not meant to be ignored.

Tim had been raised by an abusive father whose rampages left Tim with countless emotional scars. But rather than giving up, Tim had responded to his hardship by becoming a survivor.

By the time he was a teenager and was able to run away, he did. He was pretty hardened. In fact, Tim saw faith not so much as a matter of trust, but as a matter of taking charge and being tough. When he was well into his thirties, his survivor instinct carried with it a hidden vulnerability. Tim didn't know how to let go.

In time, Tim's life took some serious downturns. His teenage kids began rebelling against his heavy control. His wife, who was disabled with multiple sclerosis, grew steadily worse. Medical bills began draining his savings and Tim found he could not maintain his mortgage payment. Worse yet, the family business that had thrived in his hometown for more than two generations was now threatened by a recent highway closure.

For years Tim dealt with all these problems heroically. Whenever his business seemed doomed, he worked longer hours. When he knew his wife was having an extra bad day, he tried to be there for her. He never complained, and he never asked for help. In a sense, Tim was very brave and noble, but in reality he was running scared from emotional pain. He was deeply entrenched in the diversions of survival. Like a man bailing water from a sinking boat, he was simply too busy to allow himself to feel down, much less depressed. Instead, he lived by the saying, "When the going gets tough, the tough get going!"

With every passing month Tim found himself in deeper trouble. He was borrowing heavily from the time he needed for rest and recreation—much like a man borrowing increasing amounts of money to pay off growing debts.

One day, without warning, Tim fell apart. It seemed to start as he awoke. There was a vague but growing feeling of being overwhelmed. Slowly he began to sense his fight was gone, replaced by a sense of quiet panic and hopelessness. By mid-morning he felt paralyzed inside.

Tim soon quit going to work at all and within weeks had lost his business outright.

What had gone wrong? Why did a survivor like Tim lose it? The answer lies with unresolved emotional pain. Although Tim had been dealing aggressively with his external problems, he had failed to address his emotional pain. This subtle failure was his undoing.

Tim did what many people do who have never hit the wall of

acute depression. He assumed he could fight forever. But at some point Tim's efforts to escape his inner pain had to reach their natural limits. No one can run forever—there will be times when one cannot run at all.

Survival experiences can be exhilarating, but they can also be terrifying. Let's step inside Tim's experience, to feel what he felt the morning he fell apart. The following scenario may seem unlikely, but its intensity closely parallels what happened in Tim's world when his unresolved emotional pain finally caught up with him.

Imagine yourself tramping through a wooded mountain area far from civilization. You are weary from hours of walking. You crest a small hill and walk into a clearing. Something dark is moving off to the side. It's two bear cubs at play! Quickly you begin to backtrack. Your senses are aroused, for you have a clear mental image of just who is in charge of those cubs. In fact, you hear a crashing sound moving toward you from one hundred yards away—Mother Bear. As you run, you survey the possibility of the lower branches on dozens of trees. You are reacting more than evaluating. You know the mother bear is closing.

The approaching mother bear can be likened to a person dealing with emotional pain. The pain accumulates when you don't deal with it. One day something slows you down inside and draws your attention. Something inside is making you very uncomfortable and it demands your attention. It is the bear of inner pain. You suddenly become aware of feelings long ignored. They are not pleasant memories of better times; they are ominous and threatening. Indeed, to Tim they felt all too much like the emotions he experienced when his father had abused him as a boy.

Once the bear of pain has been stirred, the chase is on. Relentlessly it pursues us. Shortly we feel its hot breath on our neck, and we run even faster! We look for diversions in life to keep from having to face the pain. We erratically change directions hoping to avoid being mauled by terrible claws and teeth. Just as we are about to get caught, a fresh spurt of energy sends us sprinting even faster!

In our valiant attempt to escape, we discover anew the power of adrenaline and diversion. It is impossible to be depressed when a bear is chasing you through the woods. Risk is intoxicating, and in the fury of the chase, depression evaporates. In the heat of escape from emotional pain, one begins to feel much better. Adrenaline has a way of doing that. We are sure our survival instinct will pay off again. Feeling the exhilaration of escape and momentary relief from inner pain, we keep going for all we are worth.

But adrenaline is limited, and diversion always deteriorates. When we have depleted our stress-response brain chemicals, we become quite vulnerable. Exhaustion looms like a giant boulder on a narrow road, preventing our escape. Soon the truth becomes clear. The time will come when we do not have the strength to escape. Survivor or not, we will be caught.

Not everyone who is overcome by emotional pain will experience the kind of survival crisis Tim did. Although the emotions we try to avoid can pursue us like an angry bear, they may also accumulate as quietly as snowflakes on a walkway.

Suppose you lived in a remote cabin during a cold, snowy winter. In order to get your mail, you had to shovel the walkway to the mailbox every day. But one cold, stormy week you decided to put off getting the mail. When you finally opened the door, you found more snow on the walk than you could reasonably shovel in one day. If we avoid routine feelings for too long, they can pile up until we can no longer deal with them quickly, even if we want to do so.

Surrendering to Depression

When our strength is expended, when emotions are breathing down our neck or piled high on our doorstep, two results must follow if we are to survive in reasonable health. First, we must surrender. There are times we should embrace our inner pain, actually allowing the bear of depression to catch us! Second, we must go through a period of recuperation, just as we do when we are overcome by a physical ailment.

How do we surrender? What exactly happens when we run out of diversions from emotional pain and can no longer produce adequate adrenaline to run faster? The truth is, the surrender process will usually occur naturally if we let it.

We hit emotional limits in the same way our bodies hit physical limits—just like the long distance runner hits a figurative wall. In fact, the way the body signals limits is similar to the way the mind informs us that we have hit the wall of emotional pain. Consider the phenomenon known as deferred physical shock.

Gary had been enjoying his new skateboard for only an hour when his wheels got caught in the gravel, which sent him slamming to the hard pavement. In breaking his fall, he broke his arm.

Gary had his arm set and placed in a plaster cast. He returned home in time to eat dinner. Despite his mishap, Gary went skateboarding for another hour. He continued to bounce around the house in his usual way that evening. But the following morning he hardly had the energy to get out of bed. He seemed completely exhausted. What could have happened to drain his abundant energy during the night?

A heart attack victim may experience a similar energy drain. When oxygen cannot get to a small portion of heart muscle, that area dies, thus a heart attack. Only a tiny portion of the heart may be involved, and the heart can often survive the loss. Yet the victim of the injury is incapacitated for days. Even after initial recovery, the victim will still be handicapped for a long time. This physical slowdown phenomenon is caused by the effect of three interrelated factors: stress, fatigue, and neurochemical depletion.

In the case of both Gary and the heart attack victim, physical trauma to one organ forces the body to respond as a whole. All of us have probably experienced a lesser version of this phenomenon. We work day and night preparing for a special event such as a wedding. We run on our deep reserve, pushing ourselves without thought for tomorrow. Suddenly the grand event is over, and we enthusiastically attend to cleanup and other details. We breathe a sigh of relief. "It's over! The pressure is off," we say.

Wrong! The next two days we may feel lethargic and empty. We may also discover that our recuperation gets in the way of other projects we wanted to do. What has happened? We have expended the adrenaline and neurochemical reserves that help us cope with stress.

An athletic coach, aware of this phenomenon, carefully helps his athletes peak, making sure they don't push themselves too hard, or use up their stress-response neurochemicals before the big game.

A precise medical definition of this occurrence would be "stress-response syndrome with presentation of acute fatigue, represented by stress-response neurotransmitter depletion"— otherwise known as the shock syndrome. Shock automatically slows down our bodies and emotions in order to allow for recuperation. In short, it protects us, shielding us from additional pain that would come if we didn't ease up.

The shock syndrome even appears in Native American hunting lore. Hunters knew if they wounded a deer as it was running into the brush, an immediate pursuit would mean chasing the deer for miles. So the hunters stayed back until the injured deer stopped and laid down. If the arrow wound was severe, the deer would soon go into shock. Once in shock it could no longer run. Now the hunters could approach the deer, whose natural system of healing and protection had overcome its ability to flee.

The shock syndrome begins under two conditions: (1) when pain or trauma so overwhelms us that our stress-response neurochemicals are quickly exhausted or decreased and (2) when emotional trauma is followed by a slowdown in activity—such as when Gary and his broken arm finally went to bed. During the night, Gary's nervous system slowed down production of those brain chemicals that had kept him running around instead of recuperating.

The response to traumatic physical or emotional stress is much the same: Both induce a slowdown. Remember what happened to Tim that morning when he was at last caught by the shock syndrome? He didn't quit going to work because he had a bad attitude. He hadn't even stopped being tough. He simply could not pull himself together anymore. He could barely care for his ailing wife, much less work to pay for her medical bills. It wasn't just his mind that had shut down. His whole body felt lethargic. His stress-response neurochemicals were exhausted. Tim had never felt so helpless before.

Tim had a more serious problem than the lethargic symptom of the shock syndrome. He was trapped by despair. If being strong didn't work, then what hope was there? To him, his shock was nothing more than a horrible spell of depression. In his view it was clear the shock was the real cause of his emotional pain—not the result. But this assumption was a terrible mistake.

Tim's despair was not just because he felt slowed down. We can cope with those times when we feel lethargic, when we're confined to a hospital bed following leg surgery, for example. We may not feel invigorated when we are low on certain neurochemicals, but there is no harm done in feeling down.

Tim's despair came for two reasons. First, instead of accepting the shock syndrome as the slowing down process it was, he panicked and tried to fight it off. Second, because he knew instinctively he was fighting a war he couldn't win, he became gravely terrified.

The inner pain he had run from for so long was now upon him. The shock syndrome had simply exposed Tim to his real problem—avoided emotional pain. It was long overdue.

The road into the shock syndrome can be bumpy, and even frightening, because it is so hard to give in to the very pain we have been running from. It is difficult to go from survival mode to surrender. Nor is it easy to be caught by the bear of pain. The transition is made even harder by the fact that emotional pain can confuse us. Pain complicates our ability to respond to pain. Instead of accepting our emotions and the automatic shutdown that occurs when we get overloaded, our instinct is to fend it off, to avoid or deny it to the very end. But fighting depression is the worst way to respond to it.

The same people who would routinely slow down and allow an injured ankle to recuperate often try to think away an emotional injury. Instead of slowing down as they would if they were physically hurt, too many victims of emotional pain just keep running. Of course, this means their capture by the bear of pain will be simply postponed, their pain accumulating like the snow on the cabin walk.

SEVEN

REDUCING ANXIETY

"Seek first his kingdom and his righteousness, and all these things will be given to you as well. Therefore do not worry about tomorrow, for tomorrow will worry about itself. Each day has enough trouble of its own."

—Matthew 6:33–34

SIX

Coping with Depression

False Renewal

Once we have surrendered to the emotional pain in our lives, the worst of the battle is nearly over. But wait! Often, when we are just about to get caught in the shock syndrome, we turn to one last escape plan known as "false renewal."

Just as the shock syndrome starts to take hold, we sense that our desperate attempt to escape emotional pain is almost over. Like a weary fugitive, we may finally accept capture as a blessing of sorts.

Once, while driving an old truck down a freeway, I came upon a spot where the lanes converged into one, for road repairs. For some reason I remember clearly that I happened to be praying at the time (with my eyes open). I recall the presence of the Holy Spirit in the cab. Noticing that the lane of cars in front of me were stopped, I pressed the brake pedal. A tremendous bang told me that the driveshaft had snapped out. It took out the emergency and hydraulic brake lines in a moment. I couldn't even downshift.

Those were long, unforgettable seconds as I headed for a high embankment to slow down the truck. It careened through a post, nearly flipped over, then slid backward down a hill before finally rolling to a stop. It was over. I still remember how grateful I was when the chaos and immediate peril were over. I was alive and in one piece!

When our rapid descent of emotions is over, we may find some immediate relief. But a danger remains. Surrender may allow just enough relief to encourage us to once again try to resist the shock syndrome, to try to regain control over our feelings. This is false renewal.

False renewal is common in treatment programs for alcoholics, because few alcoholics start treatment before reaching the end of their rope. They often arrive exhausted and in the early stages of the shock syndrome. After achieving two or three weeks of sobriety, the alcoholic begins to feel better about life, even self-confident. Then he may start off on his own again—on the road to another disaster. This optimistic client is riding on what alcoholics affectionately call a "pink cloud." The alcoholic becomes convinced his life and problems are now quite manageable, the crisis is over, and that on second thought his emotional pain had never been that bad after all. So he resumes precisely those patterns of behavior that fed his drinking problem in the first place. False renewal is a costly trip down a dead-end street, and it isn't long before he crashes into the shock syndrome once again.

The Promise of Healing

The good news about the shock syndrome is this: It is as much a beginning as it is an end. It is at worst the end of an escape from pain, but at best it is the promise of healing.

After false renewal there is no place left to run. There is no more escape on the magic carpet of adrenaline. The shock syndrome finally has a grip; the bear that has so long been in pursuit must now be faced.

Even at this point, though the shock syndrome obliges one to feel emotions, the instinct is to stay in control of how one hurts, to control the shock syndrome in any way possible. And though it is normal to resist the shock syndrome, if a person is not careful, the struggle against surrender can become a struggle against healing.

Studies show that those victims of serious accidents or overwhelming emotional tragedy who quit trying to cope are statistically less likely to recover. But, on the other hand, failure to become vulnerable at appropriate times can also prevent healing.

Have you ever seen the recovering heart patient who won't take it easy; the anxious, bloodied accident victim who runs around in a frenzy; or the person in grief who will not stop and feel? There is a time and place for struggle, and there is a time and place for surrender.

In one well-known experiment, researchers investigated how wild rats might use their whiskers in helping their sense of direction while swimming. The first rat had no whiskers removed. When researchers dropped it into a tub of warm water, it swam for a long time before it drowned. The second rat had whiskers cut from one side of its nose. When placed in water, it swam for only a few minutes before drowning. The results were puzzling. Then the researchers learned that the lab assistant, in order to cut the whiskers, had constrained the rats in a thickly gloved hand—a process that had taken considerable time and a tight grip. The rats, realizing they were overpowered, had apparently resigned themselves to a situation of helplessness and could not bounce back for a prolonged swim.

Similarly, when rats are exposed to too much stress in the form of electroshock, they fail to produce enough of the brain chemical norepinephrine, which is necessary for coping with stress. So we have a dilemma. If the rat that was not as vulnerable lasted longer, why shouldn't we, in a similar fashion, just resist emotional pain? Why not fight off the shock syndrome? Of course, at times we should and must fight to survive. That is why God has endowed us with the rich reserve of brain chemicals, hormones, and multiple emergency and stress coping mechanisms.

But what would have happened if the restrained rats hadn't surrendered? Either the constraint would have been greater or the rats would have pushed themselves to the point of self-destruction. Life must have limits. There are times to struggle and there are times not to struggle.

Giving Up Control

One Sunday afternoon in the church parking lot, Ben Connor, an elderly man, got into his beloved but dented DeSoto. It bore testimony to his declining motoring skills. This day he took his car out of its usual place in a corner of the lot only to crash into the side of the pastor's new Buick. A crease now extended the length of the Buick's front and rear doors and one fender. If Ben had hit anyone else, he would have done as before: apologized, promised to take care of it, and driven home. But the combination of the damaged new car and his pastor's kind face somehow brought reality home. "Take my keys," he cried. "I'll never drive again!" Some observers who had never before witnessed one of Ben's close calls felt sorry for him and said, "That's okay, you just need to be more careful."

Ben slowly started to turn back to his car. But his daughter was quicker. Taking his keys, she firmly but gently ordered him to get into her car. "I'll take you home and we'll talk about this there." Ben had driven his old car for the last time. He was hurting and his dignity wouldn't allow him to say thanks, but deep inside Ben felt great relief.

The desire to be strong, well, and in control prevents us from facing life's harder side, darker moments, and emotional pain. We don't like giving up control; it places stress on both our self-esteem and faith. So when we are forced into a situation of helplessness, it can be traumatic if we don't understand how to accept it and trust God to meet our need. Helplessness plays an important role in survival, obliging us to finally face our problems, and perhaps even to seek God's help.

"You have to overcome your urges," I once overheard someone advising an addict. How much better it would have been if the addict was encouraged to trust God to keep him sober and to remove the urges as He saw fit. Instead, this addict would exhaust himself trying to control all his thought processes, perhaps trying to prove to God he was in earnest. He was heading for real trouble, because he was relying more on human willpower than simple faith in Almighty God. Urges are normal with addicts and will not necessarily cause a slip. Exhaustion caused by controlling urges, on the other hand, very well may, for additional effort only depletes our stress neurochemicals more.

In a similar fashion, those who are experiencing depression are often told they should control or overcome their depression by being positive. "Just try to think good thoughts for a while—stay busy," they're told. "Get out and do something exciting. Take a trip." Unfortunately, taking control usually means trying to stop feeling emotions, once again, by burying them. Depression is treated as an enemy rather than what it is—an indicator of stress and pain overload. It is treated as something to fear rather than something that can lead to healing.

Feelings of Hopelessness

We don't like to be slowed down, and we certainly don't like to hurt, yet it is important to tolerate depression. Of course depression is uncomfortable, but so is much of life. Pain and depression are not our enemies. In fact, if emotional pain is accepted as it occurs in our lives, there is much less chance that serious depression will ever develop. Depression has a bad reputation—unfortunately for the wrong reasons. The hardest part of depression is not that the body and mind slow down. (Again, slowing down may be uncomfortable, but it is not that bad.) The fear and despair is what's so threatening. In other words, the terror of depression is in reality a fear of the trapped and hopeless feeling that occurs from failing to fight one's way out of depression. It is the thought that to give in is to be doomed forever to dance with the bear of inner pain.

Once I counseled a woman who had spent years in mental institutions and who was in great personal crisis. I did not see her again for a few days. When I saw her next, she handed me a piece of paper with personal notes describing her experiences. She had suffered grievously from chronic depression and other disabilities. But now she was experiencing emotional freedom for the first time in her adult life. These were her first steps on the road to healing and recovery. This is what she had to say:

> You say depression isn't bad. I have a lot of trouble with that concept. I've had too many problems with depression over the years. I have been diagnosed with chronic acute depression, or major depression, and they told me that it was a bad thing. I've been hospitalized with depression and worse things that depression led to, or at least that I thought depression led to. Now I need to rethink that.

> You say depression doesn't lead to worse things. Some of the worse things—hopelessness, despair, etc.—make depression itself seem bad. And feeling suicidal comes from these things, not from depression as such. The panic that comes from the thought of facing my feelings and pain is bad. They look so awesome. I let them pile up so high. I have so much pain and so many feelings I don't like, it's hard to face them. I don't like dealing with this stuff, but I'm getting better about it. It hurts, but I do it. And if I keep doing this, the pile will get smaller. It is getting smaller. I'm in pain, but I'm not panicking. Things look bad, but not hopeless. God is taking care of me His way. I know that.

Abraham Lincoln suffered from chronic depression: "I am

now the most miserable man living. If what I feel were equally distributed to the whole human family, there would not be one cheerful face on earth. Whether I shall be better, I cannot tell. I awfully forebode I shall not. To remain as I am is impossible. I must die or be better."

"We don't like to be slowed down, and we certainly don't like to hurt, yet it is important to tolerate depression. Of course depression is uncomfortable, but so is much of life. Pain and depression are not our enemies."

One woman, Suzanne, recognized the feeling before it arrived. Every fall depression returned, and she knew it wouldn't subside until the next spring. Understandably, she felt trapped and terrorized. "If this depression would just leave," she often whispered to herself, "I would never ask God for anything else good in life."

All summer Suzanne tried not to think about the probability of her depression returning. She stayed busy. She loved to shop, even though her bills became overwhelming. Shopping made her feel better. She shopped and stayed so busy that she finally became fatigued. By the fall, Suzanne felt as though all her energy was sapped. Nothing interested her. She just wanted to lie in bed with the covers pulled close. She slept at least ten hours a night. Her job was torture, for she had to struggle to concentrate on anything she did. Her gnawing perception of internal pain always lurked in her thoughts. She felt so alone. Doing anything was a struggle; her hope had faded, only to be replaced by consuming and draining emotional pain.

Suzanne's greatest problem was not her depression. It was the fact she was overwhelmed by hopelessness. *Where will this depression take me?* she wondered. She simply did not realize that her emotional pain, which seemed so overwhelming, would not continue to increase. Having no idea that shock syndrome was there to help her heal, she instinctively struggled against it. Suzanne was at war with her depression. She could not win, but she refused to lose. If she had only quit running from her pain it would have stopped accumulating into such large mountains. Indeed, the shock syndrome that is understood so little yet feared so much acts as an emotional buffer, like an electrical circuit breaker preventing an overload. In other words, no single experience of depression can grow past a given point. Although Suzanne was forever fearing the worst—that is, having to face all her pain at once—that never happened. Instead, her worst experience was hopelessness.

Dealing with Emotions a Wave at a Time

The shock syndrome buffers any form of emotional pain, including depression and grief, by allowing felt emotional pain to arrive in "waves." In turn, each wave is limited in depth and duration.

The wavelike patterns of depression and grief are quite similar. Take, for example, Sharon, who lost her daughter Becky in a traffic accident. After receiving the news of her daughter's death from the physician, Sharon was at first stunned and broken. She soon entered shock. Upon arriving home from the hospital she tried to steady herself. "What do I need to do?" she stammered softly. "My family needs help." Within an hour Sharon began to call relatives and make funeral arrangements. She talked to friends and neighbors and somehow remained reasonably composed. During this crisis period, her nervous system was compensating for her stress with extra endorphins.

An hour later, without warning, she experienced a fresh wave of grief. She wept. Within an hour the grief subsided. She was numb and close to exhaustion, due in part to depleted neurochemicals. Still, she continued with some necessary housecleaning while talking to friends visiting from the church. Later, just as she was folding a shopping bag, another wave of grief struck. Her heavy grief seemed to ebb and flow up to the time of the funeral and for months thereafter. But slowly the overall intensity of her grief diminished. The shock syndrome was helping Sharon process her pain.

If grief and emotional pain did not arrive in waves, a victim of depression or grief could theoretically experience an incredible depth of emotional pain all at once, a tidal wave as it were.

Fortunately, that does not happen. We instead must process pain a little at a time.

At the same time, grief patterns themselves vary greatly. As we grieve we often feel anger, guilt, fear, compulsion, and confusion, especially if we are fighting the shock. For the first few weeks, grief tends to be overwhelming. At this stage people tend to feel they are making absolutely no progress. Mourners often battle a myriad of feelings, wondering if the sun will ever shine for them again.

All cultures have developed support systems for grieving, which function to help people through initial despair. Funerals, wakes, potlucks, all help move the grief process along. Such encouragement and hope, however, is not necessarily available for the victim of depression. Unlike a victim of grief, a depressed person will often struggle with emotional pain to the bitter end, always trying to find yet another exit from depression and succeeding only in making it last longer.

Despite feelings of despair, which is normal, depression—like grief—is not a hopeless process. Indeed, as each wave of grief or depression comes and goes, real progress is made whether it is obvious or not. The process is much like trying to empty a deep well with a bucket. For a time, every lowering of the bucket produces a full load. You do not see any progress. Only when the water level nears the bottom of the well does the bucket finally return half full. Similarly, it may not be until a month or two into grief and depression that a partial wave of grief begins to reveal progress is being made.

People need to know that both depression and grief will ease if they are only endured. Like grief, depression is not a pit; it is a valley, and God will shepherd us through that valley, no matter what its length.

Suggestions for Coping with Depression

If you are experiencing grief or depression, please take courage. Try these suggestions for coping:

Hold On

If you are hurting, the advice to hold on may sound cheap; nevertheless, it is good advice: Don't fight and don't panic.

Don't use up your stress-response neurochemicals as fast as you produce them. Don't try to force your nervous system to be up just because it has slowed down for a while. Just trust God and hold on.

Depressed people tend to give up hope too soon. This is not an advantageous move, because hope helps us wait for healing. Don't pin your hope on overcoming pain—accept it!

Consider the surfer. Surfers setting out from the beach must fight through crashing waves until they are far enough out to ride them. As they walk out and the giant combers hit them, they duck under the surface with their boards. For a few moments they are without air, whipped around in the churning water. But soon they surface and continue swimming. What the surfers experience routinely would send many people into fear and panic. To be without air, out of control, cold, and isolated would terrify anyone who wasn't prepared to be under the water.

What makes being engulfed a routine for the surfer is his awareness that if he waits, conditions will get better. He has a reasonable hope. In the same way, depression will be less fearful and will usually lift more quickly when we realize we are simply going under a wave. When our stress-response neurochemicals are depleted, they need time to replenish; they should not be used as fast as they are produced. Without hope of surfacing, it is easy to frantically fight emotional pain, thus prolonging the effect of a wave.

Process Feelings

To understand how to process emotional pain, let us look at how we process joy. When we experience a beautiful sunset, or the exhilaration of a bike ride on a crisp fall day, or the excitement of a romantic relationship, we allow that experience to soak in until our interest fades away and turns to something else.

We also need to process other emotions, or let them soak in. In order to understand why, let us borrow from the psychological principle of extinction. Simply understood, this principle demonstrates that most behavior patterns will die if not rewarded. For example, if we go to numerous movies and never find a show we enjoy, we will probably quit going. A new hit tune is exciting at first but in time loses its appeal. The best tune will not stay at the top of the charts forever. As the thrill (the reward) of the song lessens, our interest in it also lessens, eventually dying out.

For another example, imagine yourself in a lawn chair overlooking a beautiful ocean view. The sun is setting magnificently; the breeze is gentle and balmy; a cool glass of iced tea is dripping condensation onto your fingers. Now this idyllic setting might be very enjoyable, but suppose the sunset remained and you were forced to sit and watch it for eight hours straight. It could become unspeakably boring and uncomfortable. We simply cannot maintain focus on a single diversion indefinitely.

Try applying the extinction principle to your emotional pain. Allow yourself to grieve. Take time to feel your pain. If you have been chronically depressed, you probably have a mountain of unprocessed pain. Extinguishing a mountain of past pain can be quite a task. Hurrying won't help. Give yourself time.

Sometimes people wonder how much past pain they should feel at a time. The answer is simple: Feel what you can handle. Don't take on so much it overwhelms you, but don't deal with so little you don't make progress. And always process your current feelings of pain so they don't accumulate.

It is a rare moment when we stop all our diversion from pain. We fill our lives with hobbies, sports, solvable problems, projects, daydreaming, "puttering around," and any number of activities that divert our attention from pain. We divert by both choice and habit.

With all our diversions, it can be difficult to stop and feel what is really going on inside. It is all too easy to tell ourselves something we want to hear, to decide how we ought to feel or how we want to feel. It is hard to be accurate about emotions we prefer to deny—to tell ourselves that the lower brain, the emotional part of our brain, isn't feeling what it is feeling.

Our accuracy in identifying our emotional pain can be increased by practicing a simple exercise. Simply stop all diversions for a moment. Stop and experience how you feel, with no explanations or interpretations. Feel what is happening when you really stop. If you are alive, your lower brain will be feeling something. Next, identify that feeling in one simple term before it is upgraded or changed. Perhaps you feel scared, sad, angry, or you just feel good. Repeat identifying, or naming, that feeling to yourself.

Remember, emotions are natural responses. They are neither good nor bad. What we do with them is the issue. If you feel sadness or anger, let those emotions run their course. That does not mean if you feel sad you should stay sad, or if you feel angry you should yell at someone. Simply identify your basic emotion. If you are angry, make an extra effort not to let that emotion misdirect you while it is occurring. Accept the emotion you are feeling, then process it in the manner already discussed.

Don't Withdraw

Many people deal with stress and pain by withdrawing from society. Some simply decrease their involvement, while others retreat into their own inner world. Be aware that depression takes different forms. If you have the kind of depression where you tend to withdraw too much, it may help to slowly increase your involvement in activities and relationships rather than slowing down more. However, this principle does not apply to depression that is a result of exhaustion. If you've worn yourself out trying to control your external world, the best thing for you to do is to slow down.

Generally speaking, withdrawal functions as a means of hiding from problems—staying in control of painful experiences by trying to screen them out. But anyone who withdraws as a method of pain avoidance soon begins to face management problems. Don't try to organize everything in your world in order to keep it completely scheduled, orderly, and predictable. You can never build a hidden sanctuary for escaping problems: What you do build, you can't completely control; what you do control will eventually wear you down. As you tire, diversions from pain will become less effective. In the end, a world that we think we can control can become an emotional prison we soon discover to be uncontrollable.

Let God Have Control

While some people withdraw to stop pain, others endeavor to control and fix every source of stress in life.

It is difficult to relinquish our natural tendency to try to control all of the sources of stress in our lives. Nevertheless, when you notice yourself getting caught up in trying to control or fix stressful situations, try to develop the habit of letting go instead. Ask yourself, *Am I trusting God to handle the outcome of this situation or am I trying to make sure it turns out the way I think it should?* Of course there are times when we need to be responsible and try to keep situations under control. But there is a subtle difference between taking control because God wants us to and taking control because we are trying to insure an outcome we want.

Our very human tendency to control and fix our world not only wears us out but also leads to the problem of codependency (which we will discuss in a later chapter).

It is far better to trust, to accept what God wants you to accept and change what He wants you to change.

If God permits difficulties to enter your life, try to accept them as His will. Be thankful even for little things. Accept whatever rest and peace God gives you rather than trying to make everything peaceful.

Finally, make sure you are living by the Bible's standards. It is amazing how life improves if you are spiritually healthy. Beware of bitterness, resentments, selfishness, and other qualities that can make anyone's emotional health fail.

It should be noted that at times depression can cause enough trouble or be a type which requires prescribed medication and counseling. Everyone needs help occasionally. Getting help from qualified counselors need not supplant your trust in God and His help with your depression. God can use people to help us, too. God can truly control our lives—including leading us to a professional counselor or the proper medication.

Part 2: Blocked Escape Routes

SEVEN

REDUCING
ANXIETY

"Seek first his kingdom and his righteousness, and all these things will be given to you as well. Therefore do not worry about tomorrow, for tomorrow will worry about itself. Each day has enough trouble of its own."

—Matthew 6:33–34

SEVEN

Reducing Anxiety

Nancy was working at her register at the supermarket. Suddenly an overwhelming feeling came over her. *I've got to get out of here!* she thought. Her heart pounded wildly and her face flushed. Nancy felt like screaming. *Take a deep breath; breathe slow,* she told herself. *I can't lose this job, too.*

At least once a day Nancy had a panic attack. It could happen anywhere at anytime.

If you've ever experienced runaway anxiety, you know just how disabling it can be. It can cause routine activities like shopping or driving to be nearly impossible. Anxiety attacks can occur while you're conversing on the job, taking a walk in the park, or sitting at the kitchen table.

Of course, not all anxiety attacks are overwhelming; some are only persistent or occasionally bothersome. But anxiety affects everyone. Even if we have great faith, we are still occasionally vulnerable to anxiety. Consider the minister who suddenly realizes the funeral he is to preside over starts in only ten minutes across town and he doesn't even have his Bible. Or consider the housewife at home alone on a stormy night: The phone and power lines are down, the battery-operated radio reports a series of major traffic accidents on the interstate, and her husband is four hours overdue.

Sure we trust God. Yes, He is with us. But that doesn't always keep our frail human hearts from beating fast.

In physical terms, anxiety is a condition of varying levels of discomfort driven by the fear response that takes place in the lower part of the brain. It is an emotional state that is commonly associated with either apprehension or a general sense of turmoil, uneasiness, or both. It can appear and disappear in a matter of minutes, or it may linger for days. Anxiety may cause you to feel charged, on edge, or uncomfortably out of step with the outside world.

Mild anxiety is often present when something worries us,

when we're indecisive over a matter that urgently demands a response, when we are fighting depression, or even when the memory of a stressful situation surfaces. But serious anxiety doesn't appear without a reason. It starts as a very natural response to emotional and physical pain in our lives. In time, however, anxiety responses can be learned in the lower part of the brain just like other habit patterns, such as anger and addiction. Anxiety can even be triggered by memories or learned responses.

Benefits and Problems of Anxiety

Surprisingly, anxiety is as well-suited to helping us as it is to hurting us. In moderate amounts, anxiety can energize and motivate us, albeit uncomfortably. It can be crucial when we are in threatening situations. Suppose we hear the terrifying roar of an approaching tornado. When disaster is at our doorstep, we don't just sit there. We become highly anxious. All of our senses become focused, our blood pressure and heart rate increase, and our adrenaline flows. Assuming our anxiety is not paralyzing, we're ready to move quickly and decisively.

This condition is known as hypervigilance. During hypervigilance, our bodies produce hormones to speed up our metabolism, while our digestive system slows down to preserve blood for our muscles. At the same time, the liver releases stored cholesterol for long-term energy, and adrenal glands release cortisone (an anti-inflammatory) as well as causing an increase in sugar burning (for fuel). All in all, anxiety helps us cope effectively with most emergencies.

So if anxiety plays a necessary role in our lives, why can it be such a problem? The real problem with anxiety occurs when the brain declares an unwanted emergency. Under certain circumstances, when our emotional fire alarm sounds, the anxiety-response center in our lower brain can fail to distinguish between a drill and the real thing. For instance, when we experience a little stress, the lower part of our brain may respond as though we were facing a life-threatening situation, causing the release of adrenaline and other neurochemicals that make us tense and hypervigilant.

The body needs stress to function, but it doesn't need constant emergencies or excess adrenaline, especially if we are not physically active. Unwanted anxiety can harm us emotionally and physically, especially when it becomes chronic. It can also wear us down, for when we live anxiously we waste energy. We become tired. The more tired we become, the more we feel physical and emotional pain. Unfortunately, for many people this increase in emotional pain leads to greater anxiety.

One of the significant problems with chronic anxiety is the imbalance it causes in brain chemistry. Anxiety causes us to overexpend the brain chemicals that help us cope with stress. In turn, the depletion of these chemicals can lead to a lack of motivation and negative mood swings. That is why long-term stress and anxiety are often followed by depression. In addition to causing an imbalance in brain chemistry, chronic anxiety also taxes the nervous, circulatory, and digestive systems.

Besides making us alert in crisis situations, anxiety has an additional function. It serves as an antidote to emotional and physical pain.

Since anxiety is commonly thought of in connection with pain and distress, its pain-masking function may come as a surprise. If anxiety causes emotional pain, how does it also stop it? In modest amounts, anxiety is an effective smoke screen—a diversion from other emotional pain that may be occurring in our lives. Anxiety masks our emotional pain in two ways. First, it draws our attention away from what is immediately bothering us. Second, as with anger, anxiety stimulates the release of endorphins (discussed in an earlier chapter). These serve to temporarily ease both emotional and physical pain.

Suppose you're returning a defective toaster to a department store. To complicate things, you've lost the receipt. You begin to think through your upcoming dialogue with the manager in which you will ask for your money back. The idea of being hassled because you have no receipt is so upsetting that you think of returning home, but you really need a working toaster. The more you think about the impending conversation, the more anxious you feel. That anxiety works to your benefit. Suddenly you perk up and focus on what you'll say; you acquire a certain edge. The upcoming encounter now seems more manageable.

What happened? Mild anxiety has partially masked the fear of confrontation. It would work the same with a difficult and pressing financial problem that needs to be resolved immediately. Notice how you become more focused and intense as you try to find a solution? Your anxiety response is at work. We constantly use such mild anxiety to our advantage.

Anxiety would be a wonderful coping mechanism for emotional pain except that it is not very controllable. Anxiety can get away from us and in the end create more problems than it solves.

When Anxiety Gets Out of Control

Once we have discovered the helpful side of the anxiety response, we can learn to induce it at will, intentionally placing ourselves in a mildly anxious state. We perpetuate the process by becoming physically tense, purposely worrying, having anxious thoughts. But such anxiety for convenience is an unhealthy habit.

Furthermore, if we have an abundance of emotional pain in our lives, we may come to rely too heavily on anxiety as a pain-masking tool. In time, our increasing anxiety may begin to hurt as much as the pain it is meant to mask. A vicious cycle ensues as we use more anxiety—with less effect—to mask more pain. (It should be noted here that anxiety patterns can also be caused by circumstances beyond our control.)

Here's where the trouble begins. When we find anxiety has served us well in a particular situation, such as returning a toaster or masking pain, we may deliberately use it again. At this point our lower brain begins to record our response. Soon, an imprint, or habit, develops and we have learned anxiety. In time, anything triggering these learned patterns, or imprints, will produce the anxiety response. Stress cues, each of which triggers its own anxiety imprint, differ from person to person.

Once our emotionally-driven lower brain has learned anxiety, we are in a danger zone. In fact, for some people the anxiety response may recur spontaneously. There is no way of directly controlling response patterns learned in the lower part of our brain, no off switch we can use to terminate our anxiety responses. Moreover, a variety of situations can trigger previously learned anxiety responses. Eventually, emotions, pressures, or just the memory of a past anxiety may cause learned anxiety to occur.

My father told me the story of an elderly woman whose lower brain learned an anxiety imprint in two unforgettable minutes. When he was a boy, this woman took him to a famous exposition in San Francisco. She noticed a great wooden structure advertising itself as the Scenic Cruiser. "What a lovely train ride!" she said, leading my father by the hand. "Come on. It's a great way to see the view." They eagerly rode the "train" to the high point of the track. He (as well as she) never forgot the moment they reached the top of the first and highest drop-off—for it was in fact a roller coaster, not a train. A terrific view indeed was before them. "Look over there," the elderly woman began, "you can seeeee—"

The adrenaline-producing, bone-jarring ride caused the woman an immediate anxiety attack. Even after the ride was over and the two minutes of panic had ended, the mere thought of the ride brought her a surge of anxiety. She carried that vivid experience with her the rest of her life.

Learned anxiety, such as the fear of roller coasters, cannot be reversed. That is to say, anxiety cannot be unlearned. Learned responses stay learned. It's like telling a child who has just awakened from a nightmare in a dark room, "Just stop shaking." The child doesn't want to be scared, but once the anxiety and fear imprint in the lower brain has started, it tends to run its course. It takes time for the fear to be weakened.

Adults and children have similar problems with anxiety. Nancy, who had the panic attack while she worked at the supermarket, saw her panic attacks begin with the death of her husband. She had become apprehensive after her young husband's first heart attack. She feared it was only a matter of time before he experienced another. The months of waiting wore her down and, as she suspected, one day the second heart attack occurred. It was a massive heart attack and nothing could be done to save him. As Nancy waited for the paramedics, the pent-up stress seemed too much to bear. She wanted so badly to scream in terror at the top of her lungs. As she later told me, "I was terrified that if I screamed I could kill him." Nancy was in a traumatic double bind. The scream stayed bottled up.

It was soon after the funeral service that Nancy started her long struggle with anxiety attacks. They went on for years. It was not until much later, when she had processed the emotional trauma of her husband's death, that she broke free from the anxiety attacks. Even though the difficult memories lingered, Nancy eventually learned to turn them over to God.

It isn't just dramatic situations that start anxiety patterns. They can also come from chronic stress. For instance, a few months at work under a harassing foreman can cause stress and anxiety that may continue to cause apprehension long after the obnoxious foreman is transferred. Ignoring such learned responses will not help, but neither does resisting them. In fact, any efforts to stop anxiety may only aggravate the problem.

Breaking the Anxiety Pattern

There is hope, however. New and healthier response patterns can be learned in our lower brain to supersede the unhealthy ones. But it can't be done all at once. Although, as we have noted, there is no off switch for anxiety, its effects can fade with time. And beware, for they can also come back. Anxiety can be overridden for a while, and it can sometimes be diverted, but again, learned patterns don't just disappear from our brains.

There are many practical methods that can be used to break the destructive pattern of learned anxiety. Before considering them, we need to make sure our response to emotional pain is healthy.

We must accept the presence of emotional pain in our lives if we are to handle it in a healthy manner. If we rebel against the presence of pain and difficulty in our lives, we end up rebelling against the world God created. In truth, if we try to control all our pain and stress, we are attempting the impossible. We might as well try to move Mount Everest with a toy shovel!

Therefore, the best solution for our emotional pain is to accept it and then trust God to manage it. That leaves us the challenge of trusting God rather than the task of changing the universe. Following are some specific tools to help with anxiety.

Acceptance

Accept the pain that caused the anxiety in the first place. Take time to grieve over life's losses and hurts. Such grief is not a matter of feeling sorry for yourself or being overly dramatic about emotional discomfort; it is simply feeling the pain that is already there and allowing healing to take place. Grief is not self-pity, and it does not lead to hopelessness; instead, it bears the fruit of enduring hope.

Your struggle with anxiety is also a source of stress that needs to be accepted. Feel your anxiety every day, a little at a time. Let the law of deterioration (see chapter 9) work for you. Remember, some anxiety is a normal part of life and anxiety attacks can be simply too much of a good thing.

Notice how your anxiety peaks and then decreases in intensity. The peaks last a comparatively short time, so don't focus on them as though they will last forever. Watch your progress with anxiety as a whole.

Physical Symptoms

Pay attention to your body's response to stress. Do your muscles tense? Does your heart rate soar? Does your mouth go dry? When you feel these symptoms, remember that your body is simply demonstrating a survival skill, whether or not there is a real danger present. Try to accept these uncomfortable physical symptoms without compounding them by convincing yourself that something terrible is going to happen.

Patience

Feeling your pain and accepting it will help your anxiety decrease. But not right away. The lower part of your brain needs time to learn a new set of responses to stress. Each day that you accept pain in a healthy way, your anxiety problem should decrease, if only a little. Don't fight anxiety. Give it time.

Relaxation

On occasion, it is good to stop and relax. Take time to notice how your muscles feel when you are relaxed. If you tune in to your body like this you can help your lower brain learn relaxation in the same way it learned anxiety.

Because of learned behavior, frightening thoughts will lead to increased anxiety. Of course you can't repress or control all negative or scary memories, nor should you. But be careful about purposely or habitually dealing with frightening thoughts when you feel especially vulnerable to anxiety.

Faith

Seek to trust God more. It's easy to say we trust Him, but it's another challenge to do so daily. Trusting Him does not necessarily remove problems, or even stress; it simply means we will only go through what we are supposed to go through, and that God will be with us.

We do not earn our escape from anxiety. Escape is a gift. Just as salvation cannot be purchased, neither can recovery from many of our problems; they carry a price we cannot pay. Recovery is a gift from God that we receive by turning our anxiety over to Him.

EIGHT

UNDERSTANDING ANGER

"Better a patient man than a warrior, a man who controls his temper than one who takes a city."

–Proverbs 16:32

EIGHT

Understanding Anger

"You could have just taken a minute and brought my car up first. My car was closest," Paul complained loudly to the parking lot attendant. He snatched his keys from the attendant and jumped in the car. As soon as his wife got in, he sped away.

Paul's wife was embarrassed by the episode. She asked, "What's bothering you?"

Paul retorted, "Well, that attendant should have served me first. He deserved what he got."

Usually Paul was a reasonable guy. Rarely did he get excited over something as trivial as the order his car was retrieved in.

His wife was on the right track. Something was bothering Paul. He had a bad headache and he wanted to get home so he could lie down. Because of the parking attendant, he knew he would have to fight his headache five minutes longer. Five minutes can seem like fifty when your head is pounding. Paul was having an encounter with pain, and that pain was fueling his anger. In turn, anger brought out a very different Paul.

The Diversion of Anger

Anger helps us cope with pain in two basic ways. First, it causes a physical response. Our bodies become tense and excited. That tension produces lower brain excitement and induces the release of adrenaline, endorphins, and other nervous system chemicals. Their invigorating effect quickly makes us feel better for a time. Another role anger plays is that it can divert our attention from the pain we may be experiencing, both physical and emotional.

The screening effect of extreme anger often occurs during violent encounters. Notice how two people who are approaching a fist fight will first arouse their anger. Anger doesn't help them fight better, but it does increase their courage and makes it hurt far less when they take a blow.

One evening I came upon a confrontation just before one man stabbed another. As the men repeatedly threatened each other, their rage grew. Sirens were blaring just around the corner. But surprisingly, the stabbing didn't occur until after the police car had arrived. The police witnessed the attack. When the attacker's adrenaline and anger dissipated, he probably regretted the timing of his violent act. But it was too late. He had forgotten about the police; anger had clouded his thinking.

Prisoners frequently use anger not just for confrontations but as a means of coping with confinement. Prison cells and prison life cause emotional pain; it hurts to be locked up. For this reason, many prisoners use anger to focus their attention away from their cells. First, they direct anger at a person, place, or thing, then they stoke that anger as carefully as one would fuel a fireplace on a winter day. Soon they are more concerned about their "cause" than their confinement.

At one time or another we all use anger to cope with pain. For example, have you ever noticed how easy it is to clench the steering wheel of your car when you're in a hurry and get caught in a traffic jam? Have you ever tensed up when someone cuts in front of you after you've been waiting in line for a long time? What if someone thoughtlessly opens a car door into your new paint job? Anger is a reminder that pain is constantly with us.

When we are under stress and experiencing emotional pain, it is very natural to respond with anger. Even though anger may help us defeat opposition, it isn't necessarily healthy, nor is it always appropriate to exhibit. Although anger is a necessary part of life, it is also easy to abuse, and usually to our own detriment.

Physical pain often translates into anger. Think about what happens when you burn your hand on a stove. Instantly, the back of your hand turns an angry shade of red. Your response is immediate and predictable. You quickly yank your hand away, and an intense cry squeezes through your clenched teeth. Your whole body is tensed, bent, and moving in all sorts of ways in an attempt to ease the acute pain of the burn. You use both angry verbal expressions and physical movement to deal with the excruciating pain. All these responses are similar to those we use to respond to intense emotional pain.

Controlling Pain with Anger

Why do we respond to pain both emotionally and physically? The emotional response distracts us from the pain. The physical intensity not only competes with the experience of pain, but it also causes the release of painkilling endorphins. There are several methods people use to express anger and gain temporary control of pain.

Intensity

Have you ever known someone who always looks like a volcano about to explode? Such intensity indicates their anger response system is hard at work, masking stress and pain.

"Have you ever noticed how easy it is to clench the steering wheel of your car when you're in a hurry and get caught in a traffic jam? Have you ever tensed up when someone cuts in front of you after you've been waiting in line for a long time? What if someone thoughtlessly opens a car door into your new paint job?"

For many people such intensity is a way of life. I worked with a man, Gerald, who grew up in a home where someone was almost always angry. Rage was an everyday coping mechanism and Gerald learned it well. It had taken years for him to outgrow some of the anger habits he had learned. Although he made progress in dealing with his rage, he did so by replacing it with personal intensity. He seldom verbally assaulted anyone, but he was still tightly wound.

By switching from rage to intensity, Gerald's ability to cope with life improved, but, sadly, his intensity created new problems for him. People tended to mistrust him, and he suffered with high blood pressure and other stress-related problems. Gerald was a good man with a good heart; he was neither mean nor dangerous. Nevertheless, he intimidated people. They always suspected he was angry at them or about to explode simply because of the intensity etched on his face.

The Slow Burn

We all know people with chronic maintenance anger. Their anger doesn't flare, it smolders. By using anger sparingly but constantly, slow burners get tremendous mileage from little issues. Why do people do slow burns? Because rage doesn't last long enough for them. A slow burn is simply a creative way of making adrenaline last longer. Whereas rage soon spends itself, slow burns can ease moderate emotional and physical pain for very long periods of time.

Even so, a slow burn can't last forever. Neurochemicals that support the anger response must eventually dwindle. Then the slow burner is obliged to wait for his physical and nervous system to replenish so he can get his slow burn started again.

Frustration

Many people argue that they rarely get angry; they just get frustrated. Frustration, however, is not only a form of anger; it is a control problem as well. Frustration occurs when anything gets in the way of one's intentions.

It stings when even the smallest intentions are dashed. For example, we experience frustration when we're late for an important meeting and someone is driving slowly in the fast lane so we can't get by, or when we are about to have visitors and our child tracks mud across the freshly cleaned kitchen floor. Frustration occurs whenever our expectations of how life should be are thwarted.

Exploding

Have you ever known people who occasionally blow up, not caring where they are or who may be listening? They can turn any situation into high drama.

Ted was an alcoholic as well as a "rageaholic" who had chronic arthritis. In his early treatment, Ted repeatedly vented himself with wild outbursts. He would become angry at the least problem. Even a lost object or a jammed ballpoint pen would set him off. When that happened, reasoning with him was nearly impossible. It was like trying to maneuver a rowboat in a hurricane.

Without realizing it, Ted was showing what is called *learned* behavior. As with his other addictive behaviors, he had learned anger responses in the lower part of his brain. How did this happen? Years before, Ted had slowly built a dependency on anger. When he became angry, his nervous system released cortisone, endorphins, as well as brain chemicals that temporarily eased his physical pain, and even freed his arthritic joints in the process. These changes gave him a false sense of physical well-being. He not only felt better physically, but also emotionally. With this kind of quick reward, his anger soon became a habitual response.

Although Ted received a rich reward for his anger, he also ruined countless friendships in the process. This caused him even more emotional pain. After his adrenaline high left him, he felt depressed, and that was always his perfect reason to drink again.

Self-criticism

Have you ever put yourself down? It is possible to turn the cutting edge of anger on ourselves. "Boy, that was stupid!" you hear people mutter to themselves after making an obvious mistake. In reality, self-criticism is simply anger turned on ourselves to cover emotions. Such anger can take the form of criticism, negative feelings, or even rage and physical intensity, all of which are turned inward.

Self-anger patterns often pass from generation to generation, since those who criticize themselves are commonly repeating just what they have learned from parents or family members who criticized them in the past. Some adults are still trying to please their parents who said such things as, "What's wrong with you?" or "Why did you do that?" They may continue to talk to themselves in the same way: "What's wrong with me?" "Why did I do that?"

The victim of self-anger may, like any angry person, actually feel better for a while. But he must hurt himself in order to mask his pain. That is not a productive equation. As a result, chronically self-angry people are sure to become defeated and depressed.

Overachievement

Have you ever known someone who could never slow down? Such workaholics and overachievers are often hiding anger as well as pain.

Many people who are intense, hardworking, and success-oriented are driven by the physical side of anger. Their physical and nervous response system (sympathetic nervous system), which produces adrenaline, is always fired at a low level—much like the slow burner. They achieve goals with a vengeance. Such people aren't really vengeful or vicious; they are simply driven by intensity of mind and body—the physical side of anger. Their anger eases the painful stress they encounter in the process of achieving difficult goals. Unfortunately, their body anger also causes stress for them and their families.

Resentment

Have you ever had trouble letting go of past injustices? Such resentment is sometimes referred to as "cold anger," or anger after the fact.

Resentment effectively masks past pain for a while. And it may give the illusion we're really dealing with past pain. But by fueling anger, resentment only anesthetizes and perpetuates remembered pain.

Ironically, resentment probably hurts the resenter more than the person being resented, because resentment doesn't change reality. In fact, the person being resented is often unaware of the resenter's bitter feelings.

Resentment is extremely addictive because, as with all anger, it can be learned in the form of imprints in the lower part of the brain. Addiction to past emotional pain happens when painful memories return accompanied by old feelings of anger triggered in our lower brain. The problem is that although we may try to be noble and forgiving of past injustices, our lower brain does not forget. This creates a serious problem for anyone trying to forgive the past.

Penny has an alcoholic mother. For the past twenty years her mother has been drunk and disruptive on every one of her birthdays. Her birthdays are an embarrassment, a nightmare, hardly a time of joy. As a young adult, Penny has forgiven her mother countless times. Even so, whenever her birthday approaches, the memories and resentments resurface. Penny feels like she hasn't really forgiven her mother.

In fact, Penny *has* forgiven her mother. Unfortunately, that forgiveness doesn't remove emotional scars and painful memories the lower brain still remembers. Penny is now learning that forgiveness isn't a magic wand. Forgiveness is ongoing. It is to continue to grieve and process painful, learned memories whenever they arrive.

Conflict: a Source of Pain

As the saying goes, Where there is smoke there is fire. In a similar way, where there is anger, there is pain. Whenever you are mad at someone, rest assured emotional pain is moving you. A good place to start looking for the source of that pain is conflict.

Humans always bring their own emotional pain into relationships. How does this occur? When a person in emotional pain talks to someone, he likely expects support or understanding. Of course, it's possible that the person being talked to may feel imposed on, especially if too much is expected or he himself is also hurting.

While it is easy for two people to lean on each other, it is difficult for them to meet one another's needs at the same time. One of the two usually receives less support and feels unappreciated.

Consider a late-night argument between Ed and Bonnie Miller over the simplest of household chores: replacing the toothpaste cap. Ed left the cap off again. Bonnie is upset at him because he forgot. He is upset at her because she asked him to remember. The real problem, however, is not the toothpaste cap. Why did the fight occur? The clues are subtle. This family lives comfortably in a traditional middle-class home. With three children and a fourth on the way, Bonnie is under constant stress trying to keep her home in order, cover her responsibilities with the Women's Missionary Society, and look after an ailing mother-in-law. The morning sickness doesn't help either.

It would be enough, she thinks, *if he would just take care of the few things I ask, like the toothpaste cap.*

It's not that Ed doesn't want to do that simple thing, but he too is tired and distracted at the end of the day. He inevitably forgets to put the cap on, and soon the toothpaste cap war is on again. This is a family ensnared by stress and pain.

When Ed fails to recap the toothpaste, it symbolizes for Bonnie his apparent lack of concern about maintaining the home and respecting her desires. She is hurt and feels certain he doesn't care.

Similarly, Ed is hurting because of his stress, especially after working long hours for low pay and then having to fend off the tax auditor by himself. He is thinking about unwinding before going to bed. In fact, he has a headache and would like to lie down immediately. Unfortunately, since he is away all day, Ed is oblivious to many of the problems at home. To him the solution is simple. He needs only a gentle reminder now and again. He would be happy to put the toothpaste cap on and to clean the sink, but he just doesn't think about it in time. He assumes when Bonnie complains she is being critical and insensitive to his stress and pain.

Anytime Ed and Bonnie get embroiled in conflict, they can comprehend only their own viewpoints. They speak only from their own pain. They don't hear each other.

It doesn't matter who's right. At the root of this conflict are two people who are hurting and need help with their emotional pain. This couple has learned to respond to pain with anger. With that anger comes blame and justification rather than an understanding of the stress and pain that takes such a heavy toll on both of them.

Because the law of deterioration dictates that any escape from pain must wear thin over time, Ed and Bonnie have a problem. They must fix their problem with even more anger. In time they make some rather uncomplimentary comments to each other in the toothpaste cap debate. Since they need more anger to mask their most recent conflict, they will tend to pull still further away from each other and do a slow burn.

Although Ed and Bonnie felt better once they vented their anger, it was only a temporary fix. The causes of their pain remain. Soon, the marriage itself will become the victim of learned pain as the conflict becomes habitual. The conflict between them will recur, again and again.

Suggestions for Coping with Anger

Anger is simply not the best way to cope with pain. Yet, too often, we are encouraged to make the expression of anger a goal in itself. Chop wood, count to ten, yell in a pillow, get assertive, express your anger, get it out, we are told.

Conventional wisdom also encourages the regular expression of anger to keep it from mounting. Although repressing anger or letting it mount is certainly not healthy, neither is using it abrasively to avoid dealing with pain. Identifying anger is not enough; expressing it is not enough. We must learn to respond honestly and responsibly to our pain. There are some tools for dealing with chronic anger:

Have Patience

Be aware that long-standing habits of anger are not likely to change overnight. The lower part of your brain has no way of forgetting your anger responses just because you wish to do so. Nevertheless, the longer you handle anger in a healthy way, the less hold your old habits will have on you. Be patient and give yourself time. If you try too hard not to be angry, you may only increase your stress and trigger learned anger responses all over again.

Allow Yourself to Grieve

Since anger is an indication of emotional pain, use anger to alert yourself to the fact that there is a painful memory or experience you need to take time to process. If you find yourself hurting, grieve until the pain has eased. When you have done this, you may find your need for anger is gone.

Keep Your Anger in Perspective

The next time you feel angry, accept the feeling for what it is, a physically based emotion, and go ahead and feel your anger without blaming or criticizing. Don't push this natural emotion away. Let it come and go without getting worked up over it.

Forgive Beforehand

Remember that life is hard. All of us will make mistakes and offend people. In turn, others will make mistakes and offend us. So anticipate conflict and trust God for whatever He may bring. Forgive people ahead of time. Don't become angry trying to control people and problems that were never under our control in the first place.

Be Responsible

The Bible tells us, "In your anger, do not sin" (Ephesians 4:26). In responding to pain, we will always have anxiety, tension, and even anger. But it is unhealthy to turn that anger on ourselves or others simply to cope with life. Too often anger is a way of distributing our pain to others. Anger can be a means of causing others (or ourselves) to pay for our unwillingness to accept emotional and physical pain.

Of course, at times, we will become angry. Humans are designed to respond to stress with anger. Anger, like grief, is not a sin. But rejecting the pain that God has allowed by passing it on to others is sin. If others are forced to pay for our rebellion, the spiritual tragedy of our irresponsibility toward pain is only perpetuated.

We must become aware of our feelings so we can understand our anger and handle it responsibly. Rather than cast blame and create yet another victim, by faith we must accept our pain, assimilate it, process it, and grieve over it when necessary. If we receive God's grace for our personal pain, we will be less likely to lash out in anger at ourselves or others. And we'll take one more step toward emotional wholeness.

Part 3: Imprisoned by Pain

NINE

COMPULSIVE
BEHAVIOR

"I do not understand what I do. For what I want to do I do not do, but what I hate I do."

—Romans 7:15

NINE

Compulsive Behavior

A Vulnerability to Compulsive Behavior

Human behavior under stress can include overeating, over-controlling, overspending, overworking, oversleeping—anything that we overdo that contradicts our better judgment. Sometimes compulsive behavior merely complicates our lives; in its worst form, however, it can bring destruction. Compulsive behaviors happen to everyone: We worry too much and too often, or we push ourselves too long or too hard. Sure enough our overdoing behavior often is one more way of avoiding emotional pain.

So how do we get from emotional pain to compulsive behavior? How does stress lead us into difficulty? To explain how people get into trouble with compulsive behavior, we must look at the behavior that results from unhealthy responses to emotional pain.

Consider the problem of compulsive substance abuse and the kinds of people affected by it. Statistics show that in general the most intelligent, successful, and educated people get in the worst trouble with chemicals.

"Wait a minute," people ask me. "Do you mean the drunks downtown are educated and successful?"

Not exactly. Skid row represents only the smallest category of substance abusers—3 percent! In other words, most alcoholics are out making a good living.

Or consider the problem of adultery. Many outstanding Christians have been caught in the trap of compulsive adultery, and other relationship failures, thus destroying their churches and families. Such entanglements may very well occur at some difficult or vulnerable point in a person's life, and they happen far too frequently to be passed off by saying, "Oh, he or she wasn't a real Christian anyway." That is not for us to judge. Besides, a definite irony exists. Quite often the most committed Christians find themselves mired in compulsive behavior—a pattern of behavior that parallels that of the substance abuser.

Accumulating Pain

Compulsive people tend to be strong individuals; unfortunately, it is their strength that often works against them, by setting the hook of addiction deeper. The bigger and stronger the fish, the deeper the hook sets. Our first clue in understanding compulsive behavior is the desperate way we attempt to escape the hidden pain in our lives.

Take, for example, the true story of Bill Perry.

Bill Perry, at age forty, had been pastoring for sixteen years, and finally his church was starting to grow. Because of his deep faith and commitment to Christian service, Bill had poured his life into the ministry. His vacations were few and far between. On those nights when he wasn't overseeing some church activity, invariably the phone would ring for counseling, visitors would come by, or he would bury his face in books preparing for his next lesson or sermon.

Competition among neighboring churches was stiff. If Bill did not perform well in his church, certain parishioners would be inclined to drift to other churches. He knew ministers like him were often unseated if too many parishioners drifted away. His pay was low, and demands unending. Still, he was content to pour out his life as a servant of God. By anyone's standard he was a decent, honorable man.

As time passed, Bill ran into more problems. Each day the ring of the phone signaled another challenge, typical of most churches. One day his wife, Sarah, called with her own complaint: "Bill, I'm really worried. You're away from home all the time now. When are you going to spend time with the family? Our kids are growing up without you. I'm beginning to forget what it's like to have a husband. You've got to do something right now."

The anxiety in his wife's voice jolted Bill into action. He knew if he didn't do something, there would be real trouble at home. "Don't worry, honey," he said. "Let me reschedule some appointments so I can get home early this afternoon."

Wanting to do the right thing, Bill began to spend more time at home. But when he did, church morale began to wane. When he attempted to bolster the church, he failed a little at home; when he again attempted to bolster his home, he began to fall behind at church. While he experienced increasing stress and pain, he continued to be so giving that he never stopped to consider, much less deal with, his growing fatigue and the inevitable hurts that come with pastoral ministry. He quietly carried the weight of unreasonable expectations, failures, criticism, and his inability to meet all the needs that pleaded for his limited time and attention.

The effects of stress and emotional pain would not simply come and go. They accumulated, along with the many inner scars they created. Over the years, Bill's emotions had been badly scarred. He was like a battle-weary soldier, more concerned for his troops than for himself. He, who had so often carried the wounded, could not stop to tend his own injuries. Instead he began to take care of himself by running faster, living life in a blur, and diverting his attention from the relentless pursuit of emotional pain.

One Tuesday the church secretary was off sick and the receptionist had scheduled a morning dental appointment. As Bill wondered how he would compensate for being short-staffed, the office phone rang, interrupting his thoughts. Sharon Simpson, the church organist, was calling.

"Pastor, is the new choir music in?" she asked.

"Yes," Bill said and, without thinking, added, "I'll have the secretary bring it right over."

"Thank you," Sharon said. "That would be great."

As soon as he hung up the receiver, Bill remembered the secretary was out and so was the receptionist. *No problem,* he thought, *I'll take it over myself.*

When Bill dropped off the music, he stopped and chatted with Sharon for a few minutes. She was a kind, caring woman, who had lost her husband two years earlier. Her gentle voice conveyed genuine warmth and support. She wasn't demanding anything; she wasn't catering to him; she was just caring and listening. Bill could hardly remember the last time someone had so encouraged him—it felt good.

Unwittingly, Sharon had provided Bill with desperately needed relief at just the wrong time; she had given him a temporary but refreshing escape from the constant stress and emotional pain in his life. For those few minutes Bill's thoughts were diverted far from his troubles; he felt no pain.

Bill never imagined their innocuous conversation could be so dangerous. Unfortunately, this brief encounter ignited a relationship that slowly intensified into something that began to consume their lives. In the end, the relationship burned out of control, leaving in its path his ministry, his marriage, and his credibility in the community. How did this happen? Why would a minister of the gospel give up everything for an affair with one of his parishioners? What fueled one tiny spark of disaster that first morning the couple talked alone?

Bill Perry was vulnerable to the trap of compulsive behavior, in part because he wasn't accepting the emotional pain he experienced in life. Instead, he unwittingly chose to alleviate it temporarily.

The Law of Deterioration

There was another problem with Bill's choice to divert his pain. It's the law of deterioration, which means any effort to avoid pain by any form of diversion will yield diminishing results with repetition or the passage of time.

Deterioration is everywhere. The taste of a juicy steak, for example, pales if a bite is allowed to sit too long in one's mouth, and the most delicate chocolate mousse turns to mush if it is not soon swallowed to make way for another spoonful. Even the excitement of a tropical vacation has to wear off in time. If we stay too long at Waikiki, we are no longer on vacation. We'll be paying taxes there, too! We constantly search for new and better diversions. Regardless of a diversion's effectiveness, it is always followed by deterioration.

Imagine a ride on a supersonic fighter plane. What an exciting experience! Your heart pumps wildly as you are strapped into the navigator's seat. The engines whine to life and you move toward the takeoff position. Your throat goes dry. Seconds later you watch the runway fall away with awesome swiftness. The view is breathtaking. The experience of racing above the clouds at the speed of sound and feeling the awesome G-forces contorting you inside your pressure suit would probably be etched in your mind for the rest of your life. Certainly such a ride would be a diversion from the cares and pains in your life! At sixteen thousand feet you wouldn't be concerned at all about financial problems.

But if you flew in the same fighter two hundred times a year, the ride would become much more routine and the cares and pains of life would soon begin to return to mind even during flight. Diversion deteriorates—whether it is in the cockpit of a jet fighter or the busy office of a church.

Certainly, one of the most effective temporary antidotes to pain is diversion. Bill Perry's life was so busy that it was, in fact, a constant diversion. For a person who cares and loves people, ministry—despite its crises—can be a very exciting and positive diversion. Ministers pump adrenaline, too!

But remember the law of deterioration. Almost everything there is for a pastor to do Bill had probably already done. Very little in his job was new anymore. As time passed he faced another problem: His physical stamina slowly waning, and thus his ability to use activity as a diversion from pain growing constantly less effective.

Anyone who uses recreational drugs has experienced the law of deterioration. After a high, coming down is inevitable. Not only that, coming down always ends below the starting point. To offset the new low, addicts must achieve a greater high each time they indulge. But again, each new high pays off less than the previous one. Addiction is a progressive pattern of deterioration.

Becoming Addicted to Relief

The Bill Perry who had begun as a zealous young minister was still zealous, but he was running too fast, having long since lost touch with what was going on inside him. He could have probably limped along until retirement. But that one morning when he dropped off the choir music he innocently walked into the jaws of destruction. His brief conversation with Sharon Simpson would hook him into an addictive relationship.

This is the point where people make one of the most common errors in understanding addiction or compulsive behavior. On the surface, it is more apparent how someone could become addicted to something immensely pleasurable, such as a cocaine or heroin high. But how could someone become addicted or compulsive over a simple talk with another person?

Pleasure and euphoria are not the most critical elements of

addiction. It is not simply pleasure that attracts Bill to Sharon or binds the alcoholic to the bottle. Rather it is relief from pain.

Let me illustrate how powerful relief from pain can be. There are two basic ways you can teach a dog to raise its foot from the ground. You can reward it with something pleasurable like meat (positive reinforcement) or you can reward it with cessation of pain (negative reinforcement). Imagine a dog in a cage with a metal floor wired to deliver a shock. If every time the dog lifted its foot an electric shock stopped, the cessation of pain would actually be a reward. The dog would learn quickly to raise its leg. Cessation of pain can be a stronger driving force than pursuit of pleasure.

You've no doubt heard the joke about the man who hit himself on the head with a hammer because it felt so good when he stopped. This gives us a clue about Bill Perry.

Bill was not seeking pleasure when he talked to Sharon, but their conversation did inadvertently interrupt his pain. Unknowingly, he discovered a new way to avoid pain. In terms of addiction potential—because of the great accumulation of unresolved pain in his life—Bill was playing with fire! How dangerous it can be to live without adequately dealing with everyday pain.

Bill was set up for addiction. He had no intention of getting intimate with Sharon. Yet, he allowed her to be supportive and be his friend. And he had so much unresolved pain, so many emotional scars, that his new friendship provided him with as much temporary relief as a heroin user gets from the syringe!

At this point, Bill was in grave danger of becoming trapped. He was just like the addict or alcoholic who is more interested in relieving a low or some emotional distress than in pursuing a high.

Despite Bill's vulnerability to relief from stress, the question remains: How could he embark on compulsive behavior just from that first visit with Sharon? Simply, addiction is by nature progressive. Most addictions start quietly, subtly.

In part, Bill's addiction started this way because he was not very self-aware. He was ministry-oriented and self-sacrificing. He measured his faith in success, productivity, and service. He was a doer, not a thinker. However, since much of his personal pain had gone for years without being processed, he did not realize he was emotionally needy. He was not even consciously aware of how good, or high, he felt talking to Sharon. He was unaware of the power of diversion from pain.

Bill began to visit Sharon on a more regular basis, but of course with only the best of motives. It was not that the relationship was tempting (he had little problem with temptation because he was so busy); it was rather that the relationship was addictive. Time passed, and without realizing it, he, and to some degree Sharon, slowly began to protect the pain-relieving relationship.

Already the law of deterioration was taking hold: In the months that followed, deeper conversations had to take place between him and Sharon to maintain the effect of diversion. Just as in the case of substance abuse, so with any form of emotional pain: increasing doses are always necessary to maintain relief.

If Bill Perry had used alcohol to cope, he would have probably developed a pattern of increased drinking to mask his pain. But being a Christian, he could find relief only in legitimate sources, such as a "ministerial" relationship.

Their conversations become more frequent and the dialogue more personal, and, consequently, even somewhat intimate. For a long while nothing obvious goes wrong, but then the inevitable begins.

Part 3: Imprisoned by Pain

TEN

ADDICTIONS

"A man's spirit sustains him in sickness, but a crushed spirit who can bear?"

—Proverbs 18:14

Addictions

The phone rang just as Bill Perry arrived at his office. He immediately recognized Sharon's distraught voice. "I wasn't going to call you, but I'm so worried about you—about us—that I haven't been able to sleep at all. I'm beginning to fall apart."

"I understand. I'm not doing too well, either," Bill replied.

"The problem is that I need someone to talk to," Sharon said. "I've been praying a lot lately, but I just seem to be getting more confused. I don't want to be calling you all the time, but you're the only one who understands me."

Three months had gone by, and no one in the church had reached out to help Bill or Sharon. In fact, because there were no obvious outward problems, everyone in the congregation assumed business as usual.

The passage of time had not helped; the addictive relationship was progressing. Still the imminent disaster does not arrive with fanfare. Instead, it is like the proverbial frog sitting in a pan of cold water set upon a gentle fire. The temperature increases so slowly the frog is never aware of its impending doom. Similarly, Bill Perry's relationship passed through a crucial period of formation long before both he and Sharon realized the terrible truth that they had begun an alliance. It was not that they had any intent of pursuing one another; it was only that they discovered themselves in a relationship of mutual need. They were becoming dependent upon each other for the relief of pain—his pressure and her loneliness.

Denying the Problem

Sharon hurried to answer the phone one day, hoping it might be Bill. "Sharon," Bill said, "I'm just calling to make sure you're okay. You seemed so shook-up this morning."

"I am shook-up. Here I am a Christian, and the most impor-

tant person in my life is another woman's husband. It just
doesn't seem right that we should be talking so much. But I
don't know how I'd make it if I didn't know you were there."
"I feel the same way," he said.

With the realization that the friendship had taken on a new
character, their addiction gained a stronger hold. Still, Bill—
just like the alcoholic—was not too alarmed. After all, there was
no wrong intended.

For alcoholics this is the time when denial begins—with the
first realization that they like alcohol better than they should.
The alcoholic reasons that "this time" his drinking will be under
control, or that the last time his overindulging was a reasonable
mistake. Bill and Sharon were already in denial, believing there
was no serious problem and that somehow they could see things
through if they were just wise, discreet, and persevering. They
told themselves they would be cautious.

In time, Bill and Sharon began to realize their relationship,
however innocent, might be unhealthy. But this only made it
more mysterious to them, and much more enchanting.
Innocently, they began to explore the question: "Who are we,
and why do we feel this way about each other?"

But those questions are rarely answered accurately, for neither Bill nor Sharon understood the seriousness of the problem.
Neither could imagine being unrighteous. An affair certainly
could not happen to them!

As the newly discovered relationship progressed it produced
high drama. It was as powerful and as dramatic as a first date.
This was especially disastrous, because such drama and
intrigue provided Bill and Sharon increased diversion from
their pain. More drama produced more diversion. But like any
diversion, the drama deteriorated and thus became one more
temporary answer to their deepening quest for relief from pain.

By the time Bill realized there was a problem, addiction had
already reached a crisis level. Little did he comprehend that his
newfound enemy had already surrounded his camp. Failing to
understand that addiction is progressive, failing to realize how
much ground he had lost, he did not think to seek immediate
escape. But now with each passing week, the law of deterioration required him to seek increased diversion.

"Shouldn't we be careful with this relationship?" Sharon

asked Bill at the church. "How do we keep it proper and righteous?"

"Until we figure out what's really happening, we need to be careful," said Bill. "I think people could misinterpret our friendship."

"It makes me angry that people would think anything wrong about us," Sharon said. "Do you think we're doing anything wrong? What do you feel?"

"I feel a lot of things, but I don't know what to make of them. I just know that I enjoy talking to you. I feel like I just have to have a friend."

At this point, Bill desperately needed counsel outside of this addictive relationship. But who can the minister really talk to about a problem he barely perceives? Who would understand Bill's situation? Who was safe to share with? The trustees? The deacons? His in-laws? His wife? Just Sharon. So the relationship continued and deepened.

Attempts at Abstinence

Of course the relationship could not build forever without reaching a major crisis. At some point Bill and Sharon became aware that their growing friendship was threatening the boundaries of their ethics. They sat and talked, desperate for a solution. For over an hour they discussed their situation. Together they finally concluded they were cornered. Since any romantic alliance, however nonphysical, contradicted their ethics, they made a commitment to back off.

"Let's not see each other until next Tuesday, just to give ourselves time to think clearly," Sharon suggested.

Unfortunately, the strategy for backing off was born from yet another long discussion which only served to deepen the relationship it was intended to slow down. The shared purpose of finding a righteous solution simply drew the two people closer together.

They were now in deep trouble.

Sharon knew it was Bill even before she picked up the phone. "Sharon, I want you to be praying about us. I'm just afraid our relationship is much too close. It's getting too dangerous."

With the threat of losing control of the relationship, Bill and

Sharon only struggled harder to find a reasonable solution. Should either of them leave the church? What if they just keep things low-key? Would being more careful help?

Finally, Bill, for the sake of righteousness, made a desperate bid for "sobriety." "Sharon," he said, "You know I care about you, but I just can't be involved with you anymore. I can't call you, and you shouldn't call me."

The dangerous liaison was not the only thing that rattled Bill. He was now driven by the gnawing fear that if he abandoned Sharon she might not be able to take it. Then the whole world would know. He knew he had to take the risk and leave Sharon. Unfortunately, separation would only increase their emotional pain, and true to the adage, absence would simply make their hearts grow fonder of each other.

Just like the alcoholic who tries to escape alcohol, Bill and Sharon tried to separate. Immediately they felt relief, for they had at last taken control of their lives. The great sense of relief, however, was short-lived. In a week or two Bill began to hear the recurring drumbeat of his personal pain. He was aware that relief was only a phone call away (and sometimes only a short walk away—to the organ loft). Once an addiction has taken hold, and a means of masking emotional pain has been learned, humans unwittingly put themselves into positions that beg disaster. Sharon continued to practice at the church daily. Bill, who should not have been at the church by himself, was there every day.

Like a hiker trying to extricate himself from a pool of quicksand, the harder the efforts, the quicker and deeper the descent. The more the alcoholic tries to control his drinking patterns, the more he feeds them. The more an addictive relationship is controlled, the more it tires the controller. This principle highlights another problem with addiction: Tired people are all too likely to make bad decisions.

The first trip Bill made to see Sharon after the separation was made for an apparently good reason. He needed information for the church bulletin, and it would after all "just take a minute." Of course, the result was predictable. The relationship, very quietly, was reignited.

An alcoholic may abstain for a while, think his habit is under control, and then convince himself one social drink will do no harm. Like the alcoholic, Bill believed breaking off with Sharon had brought his compulsive relationship under control. How wrong he was!

At times everyone rationalizes overeating, oversleeping, overworking, overspending, or over-anything. The alcoholic rationalizes taking "just one" social drink. The overeater picks up an extra piece of pumpkin pie. "After all, it's Christmas—and it comes only once a year." For most people the results can be uncomfortable or embarrassing. Subtle denial, however, can add pounds, kill the alcoholic, and is sure to destroy men like Bill Perry.

The familiar trail between the office and the organ loft was now back in use. Indeed, conversation and intimacy between the two soon escalated to the point that it was when the relationship first broke off. But alcoholics and addicts rarely try to quit just once. Their breaking-off pattern occurs time and again, only to be followed by renewed intensity.

On one occasion Sharon said, "Bill, it's my turn. I am going to be strong. I'm not going to see or call you again."

Inevitably, Sharon would fail too. Within a week she restarted the relationship when she called Bill for help in the midst of a late-night crisis with a neighbor.

With each return of the relationship break-off cycle, the law of deterioration tightened its grip. There was always some new drama and deeper involvement by the couple in order to achieve relief from their ever-present emotional pain. Their relationship became like a nightmare roller coaster ride, increasing speed with every turn and descent.

The break-off cycle has its limits. Denial can be deteriorative, too.

Bill could logically accept failure in his attempt to impede the relationship only so many times. So, although he was uncertain as to why he broke his first commitment to stay away from Sharon, he slowly realized he was bound to fail no matter how hard and often he tried.

The failure to even pretend to control their relationship put yet more stress and pain into the lives of these two Christians. Once Bill and Sharon realized they were trapped in a relationship, anxiety quickly built.

"Sharon," Bill said, "I know we have an unhealthy relationship going here, and I don't know what to do about it. I'm torn apart inside."

"I know," said Sharon. "We have to be very careful to help each other to not do the wrong thing."

So in desperation the two continued to build their mutual dependency. The resulting emotional intimacy temporarily met their emotional needs, but it also sealed the final outcome. Someday there would be one conversation too many. Bill and Sharon would cross the boundary of what, for them, was obvious sin: a shared gaze, an overextended hug.

Becoming Emotionally Fatigued

Suppose you built a cage for a rat. At one end you dangled a fresh hunk of cheese, and just in front of the cheese you put an electrically charged grate. Just as the hungry rat approached the cheese, you turn up the electrical charge on the grate to bring the rat discomfort equal to the pain it felt from hunger. What does the rat do? It equivocates for a while, turning first one way and then another. Finally it lies down and seems to give up.

Compare this situation to Bill's predicament. On one hand, he was driven by his general internal pain to pursue the "cheese." On the other hand, he was driven back by the painful relationship he found himself entangled in. This dilemma produced anxiety that, in turn, helped mask Bill's pain.

Since anxiety is not a long-term solution to emotional pain, Bill was clearly running out of time. So, while at first anxiety itself provided them adequate diversion, in time it became its own burden, only adding to their emotional pain.

Bill, if given help, could have still escaped impending disaster. But the invasion of another dilemma was one few escape from. It is the same dilemma the anxious rat finally faces: exhaustion through equivocation. How does this occur?

Just like the caged rat running first to the cheese to escape his hunger, and then away from the cheese to escape a shock, Bill was trapped between two sources of pain. If he went one way, he faced the destruction of his life—everything he believed in—and if he went the other, he would lose Sharon and be enveloped in emotional pain. The trap soon dominated his life.

In the wake of double-bind anxiety Bill began the process of emotionally freezing up. He longed to turn back the clock, to go back to his previous life-style. He desperately hoped that everything could be like it was before. But it was too late!

Caught between two sources of pain, Bill fell deeper into equivocation. He desperately wanted the relief his relationship with Sharon first brought him. He also wanted his ministry and career. He could not have them both, so he tried to avoid both sources of pain at the same time. He was like the alcoholic who longs to go back to his preaddiction days, and at the same time longs for the joy and relief alcohol first gave him. He will find neither. He will only exhaust himself trying to change reality.

Bill's emotions were changing directions frequently. In one moment he pondered talking to Sharon again, but in the next he feared approaching her at all. *The problem won't disappear*, he thought, *and it's just too easy to think of Sharon.* Soon he was completely mired in equivocation, struggling to cope, yet failing to deal with anything.

With time, Bill's changes in emotional direction came more frequently. Finally, it was not a matter of changing course every two weeks. The exhausted man changed his strategy every few hours, and sometimes every few minutes, attempting to escape his pain. He wanted desperately to forget Sharon but he could not. With every attempt to forget, with every change of direction, he edged ever closer to exhaustion.

Responding Subconsciously

Eventually, Bill didn't even have to see Sharon to feed his addiction; he could just think about her. Pondering a relationship that is hooked into one's feelings can be as addictive as the real thing. It is like the emotional power one feels when contemplating a loved one away at sea on a long journey; the absent person cannot be forgotten.

With everything in Bill's life focused toward his addiction, it only became harder for him to avoid thinking about his habit. Part of the problem he faced is the same for any addict. Logic was not the only force driving his emotions. He also struggled with a phenomenon known as learned behavior. Learned behavior is a special function of our memory. It is not like memorizing phone numbers or remembering faces. Rather, it is a function of the part of our brain that processes emotions. The lower part of our brain is designed for processing emotions and making survival responses, not for logic. It is from this area of the brain that we feel fear, terror, rage, anger, and even pleasure. How does it work?

If anything triggering certain emotional or physical responses is great enough or repeated often enough, that response will be learned, or imprinted, in the lower brain memory. Once any behavior or experience is imprinted, it will remain stored in the lower brain. For instance, some of the physical skill of riding a bicycle will remain stored in your lower brain even if you have not ridden a bicycle for decades.

Consider a seven-year-old girl who goes to the airport to see her grandmother's plane land but instead witnesses its fiery crash. Years later, even when the girl is well into adulthood, it will still be hard for her to fly without experiencing fear and anxiety like that of the horrible day at the airport. In time, new patterns may partially override her old fears, but her memories and fear responses won't just disappear.

Necessary for Survival

By controlling fear, anger, and other emotions, the lower brain plays a crucial role in survival. Imagine yourself making your very first parachute jump from a plane. Although you've practiced repeatedly on the ground, as you step toward the open door, your heart races and deep feelings of fear rise and press you to remain in the plane. You are at war with your lower brain. While the logical part of your brain prints out, "You've come this far; go ahead"—the lower part of your brain screams, *Stay in the plane!* With enough bravado you can temporarily block out your lower brain and go for a thrilling jump and an incredible adrenaline rush.

What you couldn't do is keep that conflict going over a long period of time. In the long run you will always lose an all-out war of willpower with your lower brain. Consider a man who physically knows how to swim, but who is so depressed he jumps into a deep pool to end his life. Whether he intends to or not he will end up swimming.

A Negative Motivator

Although designed to motivate us out of life-threatening situations, the lower brain can also motivate us in negative ways. For instance, if the lower brain has learned addiction to food or drugs, when we are under stress the lower brain will use its survival mode to drive us to overeat or use. It can motivate us to disaster.

For example, we may occasionally find ourselves overly anxious or angry when facing even a modest problem. Why? Simply because that problem triggered a learned pattern or habit in our lower brain. In response, the lower brain reacts as though a great crisis were at hand. Any crisis can awaken learned habits or patterns—whether or not they are good for us.

Everyone has good and bad habits that are triggered automatically. For example, when a dog growls, we naturally pull back and our heart races before we can even think about it. This response occurs because our lower brain has learned to respond automatically to protect us. Our lower brain is sensitive to a wide range of cues: barking dogs, sirens, loud noises. In the same way, heroin addicts have learned cues: the smell of a burnt match, triggering the desire to use. Some addicts who are without a fix will find relief by sticking an empty syringe into their veins. The cue of the needle puncture causes the lower brain to release pain-killing neurochemicals.

To the average person a bathroom carries no special interest. To a cocaine addict, a high-quality toilet seat cover can suddenly become very stimulating, simply because his lower brain remembers it as the perfect place to make "lines" of cocaine. Just the sight of good plumbing appliances can elicit the urge to use! Addicts are often not conscious of such cues; they respond subconsciously.

Learned behavior was a serious problem for Bill Perry. Almost everything became a cue for this tired man. If he glanced out the window and noticed Sharon's car, that reminded him of her. Even stress reminded him of the relationship.

Bill tried not to think of her. Unfortunately, learned cues affect us even more when we are tired, and he was emotionally fatigued. He was like the dieter who does well all day, only to overeat in the late evening when his strength is spent. The

harder he tried, the less he could forget Sharon. With each ring
of the phone he wondered if it was her.

Spontaneous Recovery

Some of our learned emotional habits and patterns may be
temporarily overcome by great mental effort in the cortex (the
"logical" part) of the brain, but imprinted emotional memories
do not simply vanish. Instead, when pushed away they drowse
like a tiger, only to awaken when least expected.

Consider the phenomenon known as spontaneous recovery. To
understand it, let's reflect on Pavlov's experiments with dogs.
Pavlov put a dog in a harness mechanism and then blew some
meat powder from a bulb syringe toward the dog's nose.
Naturally the dog salivated. Next Pavlov added a bell sound
along with the meat powder. After a number of trials, Pavlov's
dog would salivate when he heard the bell, even when the meat
powder was removed.

Next, Pavlov removed the meat powder and only rang the
bell. Of course eventually, as the dog learned to disassociate the
meat powder from the bell sounds, he quit salivating at the
sound of the bell. But the experiment is even more intriguing.
Pavlov would take the dog which had quit salivating at the bell
and leave it in a kennel for an extended period. When he
brought the nonresponsive dog back to the harness and rang a
bell without offering meat powder, the dog salivated again!

Why did the dog salivate again after the habit appeared to be
lost? The learned behavior had not really disappeared. It had
just lain dormant until it recovered—hence spontaneous recovery. Spontaneous recovery is very dangerous to any addict who
deprives himself of his addiction. At first the unwanted behavior may go away, but sometimes all too easily. It will usually
reawaken weeks, months, or years later (often at the worst of
times) more powerful than ever. Worse yet, because anxiety and
stress affect a person's lower brain response, the more the person tries to control learned behavior the more likely he is to
awaken it.

A Pleasurable Stimulus

When we are under stress, our adrenal glands trigger the production of several powerful chemical substances. In the outer part, or cortex, of these glands we produce cortisol and cortisone. These chemicals increase muscle tension and blood-sugar levels. The core of the adrenal gland produces adrenaline, which causes the release of other neurochemicals, such as norepinephrine and dopamine to help us cope with stress. These chemicals help us to feel up. The more up and active we are, the less we notice emotional and physical pain.

Whenever Bill felt romantic infatuation, his brain also produced an extra amount of a brain chemical called phenylethylamine (PEA), which causes a powerful, pleasurable stimulus much like cocaine does in some people. Again, this response is learned in the lower brain.

With the pleasurable feeling of adrenaline and PEA highs, as well as the anesthetic effect of the endorphins (morphine substances), Bill Perry found temporary physical and emotional comfort in the drama of his addiction.

At this point of addiction the substance abuser has an advantage over Bill because he has some sense of the effect of chemicals on emotional highs and the depression that follows. Men and women like Bill Perry, however, are blissfully unaware that they are already a biochemical substance abuser. They continue to get emotionally high, to overextend their nervous system's neurochemical resources, and then to descend into greater depression, anxiety, and exhaustion.

Any imprint or sensitization which is learned in our lower brain will remain for life—unless God physically removes it from us. So how can we ever overcome learned habits that hurt us? Time and deterioration can help, but the threat of spontaneous recovery of habits never goes away completely. Still, there is hope. There is an answer to this dilemma: recovery, and we will carefully investigate this wonderful resource in a later chapter.

Losing Control

Bill was well into his addiction, fighting off equivocation, anxiety, and spontaneous recovery. He was fast approaching complete mental exhaustion. He was losing control.

The addict at this point may know that an expensive heroin

habit is now failing to get him high—but he is too tired, and running too fast, to stop. Exhaustion can be dangerous for anyone. Any person who has too little sleep and is stressed for too long will fail to think clearly. In fact, extensive sleep deprivation, emotional trauma, or exhaustion—in addition to depletions of the brain chemicals we use to cope with stress—will eventually be followed by clinical manifestations of serious mental illness.

Our bodies are designed to handle stress and pain only for limited periods of time.

Healthy, fresh soldiers can fight far more effectively than hungry, tired ones no matter what their cause. Prisoners can be broken when they have been under certain types of prolonged stress no matter what they believe. No human can withstand endless deprivation and stress. At some point, values, mental functions, commitments, hope, and even close relationships will fall to human frailty. When acute addicts are tormented by withdrawal, they will steal from their own kids.

Addiction takes its final ground when its victims spend the last of their strength in a fight to the finish with their lower brain. Though the addict's will is finally broken, he may occasionally try again to resist his addiction. Without God's mercy, however, the addict's "drug of choice" will ultimately dictate every move in his life.

Veterans of Alcoholics Anonymous describe a hypothetical situation in which one puts a gun to the temple of an alcoholic who has a glass of whiskey in front of him, promising to shoot the moment he takes a drink. Even stupid people would not lift the glass. But addiction doesn't operate on either intelligence or stupidity; it turns on exhaustion and desperation. Given some time, the alcoholic will take that drink even at the cost of his life. No one can be the prisoner of a destructive habit, become exhausted, and continue to stay in control forever.

The Desperate Slide

Anxiety, equivocation, fear, and physical exhaustion took all Bill had to give. The diversion his relationship with Sharon provided had deteriorated so far that no increased emotional dosage was adequate. He could not escape his addiction, and he could not afford to get in deeper! Like a runaway wagon careening down a hill, the faster it goes the harder it is to jump off. He finally decided to hang on for the duration of the ride, to duck, and to wait for the crash.

It is inaccurate to assume people like Bill Perry and Sharon waltz off to motels just for pleasure, any more than the heroin addict overdoses just for fun. Acute addiction is ultimately measured not in pursuit of pleasure but in a tragic and traumatic escape from pain. Late in addiction, getting high is usually an act of desperation and risk.

For Bill, the last days and hours before the trip to the motel were blurred by confusion, anxiety, and equivocation that led to physical and emotional exhaustion. His stress-response brain chemicals, which he sorely needed for clear thinking, were seriously depleted. He fought failure to the very end, which only led to a more rapid cycle of equivocation and further exhaustion.

In the case of the drug addict trying to stay straight, the problem is not a motel but a local park where cocaine can be purchased. After having fought off his habit for several days, the addict begins to tire. He becomes less able to recall the reasons why he desperately wanted to quit. Finally, in his confusion, he will do anything to stop the pain! He now reaches a perilous conclusion: It is infinitely better to feed his addiction *once* to quiet it than to be constantly ruled by it. His reasoning is like the emotionally exhausted dieter who goes on a binge to relax enough to get back on his diet.

In a growing state of confusion, the cocaine addict turns his car toward the park. Relief is suddenly near, but so is danger. He knows he must turn away at all costs.

The final adrenaline rush arrives and suddenly the cocaine addict feels renewed strength and vitality. *Maybe*, he thinks, *I won't use tonight after all!* He slows the car down and quickly worries about where he should go for support. But the adrenaline rush is soon over and he continues his course. As he nears the park, a renewed panic seizes him. He senses doom, knowing the wreckage that will occur if the drug reaches his nostrils. So he turns impulsively away from the park, and floors the accelerator, speeding away on the freeway. But within minutes his emotions sink further into a bottomless chasm, followed by the pain of despair.

Even as he tries to drive away, his emotional pain looms
again, and with it the learned memory of cocaine claws at his
soul. His addiction drive, the once sleeping tiger, is now fully
awake. His lower brain is staged for the final battle. The pounding of his heart increases. He feels confusion, exhaustion, and
fear. The adrenaline causes emotional tunnel vision. Risky
behavior makes more sense. Everything focuses on his addiction.

Finally, he has no more fight. He is in emotional shock. He
rationalizes that only the thrilling destruction of a buy will stop
the pain—even if he doesn't use what he buys. Now the equivocation is over. Without thinking any further, he turns the car
around. This time he knows he will make it to the park.

This desperate scenario creates the same sort of terror experienced by a workman who has lost his footing and is sliding
down a high, steep roof, trying to avoid falling into the street
below. He digs his fingernails into the shingles to slow his
descent. He uses every ounce of his strength to keep from going
over the edge, but his body and tool belt slowly yield to gravity.
There is a limit to human strength. After a valiant effort the
workman, with torn and bloody fingers, finally slips over the
edge. Likewise, Bill Perry, emotionally exhausted, went over the
edge and drove to the motel for a rendezvous with Sharon.

For a short while the pain eased. But long before morning's
light Bill felt worse than ever. Sharon was in tears, nearly hys-
terical and crushed beneath the weight of remorse. Addicts are
masters of remorse. When the high is gone, the low resonates.
The guilt at failure is overwhelming and only adds to the pain
that has temporarily been avoided.

Still, the worst is not over. It will only be a matter of time
before the cycle starts again with renewed vigor! Despite the
addict's pledge never to indulge again, the cycle will often
return in full force within three weeks.

Trapped in Addiction—The Logic of Doom

Tragically, had people known of Bill's crisis, few would have
known how to help him. He wasn't the person everyone had
known and loved. He had changed: He was hard to reach, so
desperate! Bill and Sharon were each in their own isolated
world—even when they were together.

Worse yet, the addictive cycle was beginning again. Bill found himself trying to cope with a very anxious Sharon and his ministry at the same time. As he tired, he once again began falling prey to his addiction. He found himself like the terrified workman sliding down a roof again. The despair of sliding was consuming, excruciatingly painful, and exhausting.

Bill recognized the plight of his current course, for he had traveled this path before. He could already envision where it would end. If he had used all of his energy and couldn't stop his addiction before, he thought, what's to prevent the same thing from happening now? Why destroy himself to no avail? Bill had discovered the logic of doom.

He could no longer find the will to fight. When he approached the motel he felt like he was going to an execution rather than a tryst. In exhaustion he slid toward the edge of the "roof" again, but this time without the bitter struggle. He simply let go.

In the early morning hours of the second visit to the motel, remorse returned with a new fury. Bill felt utter hopelessness, bathed in the logic of doom. *Why did I quit fighting so easily?* he wondered. *How can I have true remorse when I knew what I was going to do before I did it? How can I honestly ask God for help? Why should I even try to stop again when I know just what will happen?*

Torn by remorse but trapped by the logic of doom, Bill could not uncover a way to turn back. *Why,* he thought, *should I fight it all over again, only to lose?* At this crucial point, he made the all-too-common decision to hide his addiction from God rather than talk to Him about it.

When people quit fighting their addiction for a period of time, they usually begin what drug addicts call a run. They lose themselves in the addiction—an act which for a while is very pain relieving. At least on the "run" they no longer have the desperate roof experience. Here the addict tells himself, "Roll the dice," which means, "Quit shaking them around. Roll them; do it now. The waiting is intolerable!"

So what could have stopped Bill and Sharon from visiting the motel again? If he had tried not to go, he would have gone. If he had given up, he would have gone. At this point the trap of addiction had sprung completely closed. Someone else would need to pry him loose.

Without God's help Bill Perry could never escape his addiction to Sharon. Even if Sharon were to disappear from his life, Bill's memories of her would linger for the rest of his life, waiting for another stressful situation or mistake to be made. Repentance could make his heart right, but it could not in and of itself change his learned habits. Repentance could not remove his vulnerability. For this reason alcoholics with years of recovery often proclaim that they are not free to live unrighteously or irresponsibly as some nonalcoholics live. For them the failure to live right means the return of old patterns of thinking, or what is known in Alcoholics Anonymous as "stinkin' thinkin'." If they don't walk with God, the tiger in their lower brains will awaken and they will surely die.

Addiction to Sin

Addiction to sin is a serious problem—not only in the secular world but also in the church. Christians are peculiarly vulnerable to compulsive sin because of their knowledge of right and wrong. They have far more anxiety when they do wrong because they know it matters. They also tend to fight their addictions harder, thus feeding the anxiety that drives addiction. But again, the problem with compulsion is more than one of right and wrong. It is a failure to understand the quicksand of compulsive sin.

A good friend, a Christian alcoholic who enjoyed about fifteen years of sobriety, once said, "Christians just don't understand what sin is." His point was that most sin isn't just a matter of making occasional mistakes. Because of its link to compulsion, sin leads us in directions we don't want to go. Unless we understand our vulnerability, we will be vulnerable. If we don't understand quicksand, we may not attempt to avoid it. If we think we don't need a Savior in all areas of our lives and at all times, we may be obliged to have our need demonstrated to us. Jesus was not only needed when we first met Him, we also need Him now!

If we assume a particular sin will never touch us, then we presume our own strength, which is surely a step toward self-righteousness. The story of the sinner and the Pharisee praying in the temple reminds us that we are better off as a forgiven renegade than an everyday sinner who ignores his faults! (See Luke 18:9–14.)

Which of us intends to murder another person under any circumstance? We wouldn't dream of it. But given the right circumstances we could, for we are not all-powerful. Doesn't the Bible tell us that if we break any law we are guilty of all? (See James 2:10.) Our protection from the temptation to gossip, overeat, steal, or murder is not a credit to ourselves; it is a gift from God. It simply means we have not been brought to hard testing in that area. It is only if we are without sin that we can throw a stone at anyone else. (See John 8:7.)

Much sin is simply moral failure. However, with some sin, such as addiction, inappropriate behavior is not just a simple, calculated decision of the will; it is to be caught in an emotional trap, an addiction to relief from our daily pain. All of us fail on some level. "There is not a righteous man on earth who does what is right and never sins" (Ecclesiastes 7:20). It is, as the apostle Paul wrote, to be unable to do the good that one wants to do. Of this dilemma Paul asked, "Who will deliver me from this body of death?" (Romans 7:24). Only the Good Shepherd.

A classic tale tells of a man who was put in a sturdy cell with the promise that if he escaped within twenty-four hours, he would be granted his freedom. He tried every trick in the book. In the last hours, using a metal shard from a light fixture, he actually broke through the wall far enough that he could see daylight—but he couldn't enlarge the hole quickly enough to escape. He was returned to his original cell. On the way the guards told him the devastating news: the heavy door to his cell had never been locked.

So it is with addiction. Our furious and desperate efforts to free ourselves prevent us from finding the escape God has provided.

Hope and Redemption

A difficult out-of-town case was once referred to me by a prominent Christian family. It concerned a marriage that had been deteriorating for several years. The couple's relationship with the church, and the faith of the wife in particular, had deteriorated. The wife, Jane, (whom I knew) wanted nothing to do with her husband. Another man had come along and off they went, setting up house in a different city. Finally, Jane's family persuaded her to see me. She reluctantly agreed, hoping my visit would convince them to leave her alone.

My initial visit with Jane was in a golf course parking lot, my attempt to avoid arousing any of her negative associations with church. The thing I most remember is how old she looked. It just didn't seem possible that anyone could have aged that quickly. Clearly she was under pressure. Everyone in her life was telling her she had to go back to her husband, but she had only pulled farther away, and now she was planning to remarry.

"Jane, I want you to know I understand what you're going through," I slowly began. "It happens to a lot of people. I'm not here to get you to do anything. I'm not going to get on your case."

Months of denying her faith and values had etched fatigue in her face. I knew Jane didn't need one more person explaining to her that her actions were wrong and how they were hurting people who loved her. She knew.

I really wanted to fix the situation and see her restored in the faith, but that desire told me how much I needed to stay out of the way. If I pushed, I would only increase her anxiety, exhaustion, and desperation. Like the woman at the well in Samaria, Jane needed truth and forgiveness, not condemnation. (See John 4:1–26.)

We talked for nearly two hours. I shared about how Christians get caught in compulsive behavior just like anybody else. I explained how compulsion worked, how we get addicted avoiding pain. Finally I saw a tiny sparkle in her eyes. "You know, that does sound like what has happened to me," she acknowledged.

Addiction now seemed to make sense to her. Nothing else explained why she felt so compelled to be with her new boyfriend (he had little to offer). Yes, she was running from pain. She couldn't let go. The more she worried about leaving the church and her family, the more she felt compelled to go! She was addicted. When Jane understood the problem, a ray of sunlight pierced her confusion and despair. Maybe she wasn't so unforgivable after all. I knew we had gained some valuable ground, but we were still far from seeing Jane healed and restored to her husband.

Jane realized that if she went back home, as she had done several times before, she would certainly leave her husband again. There was no point in pushing the situation. I knew final change was not imminent.

Our visit was obviously winding to a close and I knew Jane was waiting for an ultimatum. She was waiting for me to demand she go back to her husband. I carefully left the subject alone. Conviction of the heart belongs to God. Changing of the heart belongs to Him as well. If I had pushed, if I had tried to take control, that would have been our last meeting.

"Take some time to think about things. Don't make a fast decision," I counseled her. "Anytime you want to get together again, I'm here. If someday you want to work on your marriage, I'm sure there is hope. Whatever you decide to do, feel free to call me anytime."

Two weeks went by, and Jane hadn't called. I urged the family to leave her alone. We relinquished her into God's hands. Then came the phone call. "I'm ready to talk now," she said. Jane went through weeks of addiction recovery counseling as well as family counseling. The family is back together and doing great. Now Jane reaches out to many other people who have been caught in similar predicaments.

There is hope for you, too, wherever you might find yourself. Scripture does not tell us we are made strong when we become weak; rather He is made strong. If we think we needed a Savior once but have outgrown our vulnerability, God may show us yet again just how weak we are. But when we know that we too can fall, we are far more likely to respect the danger signs of sin and cling to God's delivering power.

In a later chapter we will look carefully at God's escape plan for addiction—recovery.

ELEVEN

RELATING
TO OTHERS
IN PAIN

"When Jesus saw him lying there and learned that he had been in this condition for a long time, he asked him, 'Do you want to get well?'"

—John 5:6

ELEVEN

Relating to Others in Pain

Pain Addicts

Carl and his family were having a rotten day at Promitory Beach. Trouble began to brew early between Carl and his oldest daughter. The twelve-year-old wandered a little too far away for the second time.

"Get over here now!" Carl hollered. "You're grounded for a month!" His face flushed from red to purple. "What's the matter with you?" he yelled. "You're acting stupid, just like your brother!"

Several people looked in Carl's direction. One was Jim. Although Jim didn't know Carl, he stood poised to take action. Carl lunged at his daughter. Jim couldn't determine if the girl had been hit, but she fell to the ground in tears.

Jim had been abused himself when he was a kid. His heart started pumping furiously. He felt terror inside, terror mixed with rage. Jim hesitated, then yelled at the top of his lungs, "Leave the kid alone!"

Carl charged at Jim and shoved him. "Mind your own business or I'll deck you!" he screamed.

Feelings from Jim's childhood welled up in him. He was far bigger and stronger than Carl. He wanted to respond to the challenge and defend himself—to "deck" him, but he felt sick inside and paralyzed. He just stood there. He watched Carl walk away unharmed, unbridled. Jim felt helpless and guilty, and he feared for Carl's children.

This kind of scene is routine for tens of thousands of American families. People living out of control are found in every walk of life. When they blow up like Carl they are often referred to as "rageaholics."

Carl was a pain addict. He was not addicted to finding pain—he was addicted to avoiding it. His way of avoiding pain was to lash out in rage and burn adrenaline. As a pain addict, or rage-

141

aholic, Carl had learned to lash out at the closest possible victim whenever he was worn down by fear, anxiety, stress, or depression. It got worse when he drank. His rage and anger were clear signals that he was running from his emotional pain. He was trying to lose them in compulsive behavior.

Carl was not the only pain addict on the beach, desperate to avoid emotional pain. Everyone in Carl's family suffered from his erratic, destructive pain addiction. It made them all sick in different ways. His daughter avoided him around the house, spending most of her time in her room. She also started running with a gang at school. His wife had stress-related illnesses. She would panic and leave the house for hours when Carl seemed tense and on the verge of violence.

Even the humiliated bystander, Jim, was a pain addict. Jim grew up avoiding an alcoholic father who beat him at least once a week. His father constantly ridiculed him and abused him emotionally.

From an early age Jim learned to freeze up inside when he was confronted. He learned how to avoid expressing and trusting his feelings. In addition, he learned how to bury his feelings, thus avoiding his emotional pain. In those instances when he couldn't avoid it, he panicked inside. Anxiety began to rule his life. He had a difficult time dealing with tense situations. After the confrontation with Carl, Jim never again felt comfortable visiting Promitory Beach. He always had an excuse for not going.

Living with Pain Addicts

People like Carl or Jim's father wreak havoc on whoever is close to them. As a result, their families are all too likely to become "infected" with a progressive problem known as co-dependency.

Codependency is a self-destructive pattern of behavior that family members (or those close to any kind of pain addict) use to cope with the addict's behavior. Simply put, it is to be caught in an unhealthy relationship with anyone whose life is running out of control.

Imagine driving behind another car on a dark and foggy night. You stay close, guided by the taillights. You stay back just far enough so that if the lead car has to stop suddenly you can slam on your brakes and stop before you hit him. There is a flaw in this strategy. As long as the driver of the first car is alert and competent, everything is fine. But suppose the driver runs off the road and into a tree. The car could stop abruptly, allowing no time for adequate breaking on your part. Unable to stop in time, you would certainly hit the car.

When a person running from pain collides with reality, those closest to him may not have time to stop. Anyone who follows too closely, trying to control, handle, or fix the addictive behavior of others, may share a collision with the same thing that destroys the pain addict.

It can be terribly stressful to be caught in a relationship with pain addicts such as alcoholics, drug addicts, rageaholics, and compulsive spenders. They can be unpredictable, easily angered, overly dependent, moody, controlling, compulsive, or chronically depressed. Most of us have had the uncomfortable experience of working or living with such people.

Patterns of Involvement

Here are some common patterns by which codependent people get involved with pain addicts.

Enabling

This term describes the pattern of those who simply try to "help out." If a person is depressed, the enabler will always try to cheer him up and in some way respond to his need. Perhaps they will shop for the pain addict, or even sacrificially supply friendship.

As a youth minister I befriended a hurting family in our church: a single mother and her troubled teenage boy. They soon wanted me to visit regularly. My responsibilities for one hundred teenagers prevented my devoting much time to the mother and her son. Furthermore, the church offered activities and friendships for this lonely family. I gently told them they needed to reach out and visit others instead of being visited. As much as I cared, I had to let them hurt or they would have become more manipulative, and I would have had to disregard many other people with more immediate problems. I had chosen not to enable them.

Blaming

When a person is in pain, he often offends those who try to help. The pain victim's obnoxious or difficult behavior makes it easy to disregard him by blaming him for all his problems. But when we cut off the pain victim by blaming him, we encourage him to become less open to getting help.

When we cast blame, we effectively say, "I don't have to help." One young, single girl had become pregnant. She had come to me for help after counseling with another minister. He had simply said, "Well, I'm sorry but now you have to pay for your folly." He felt he didn't need to do anything to help, and he didn't. This minister had evidently become discouraged through the years after dealing with other compulsive people. When he gave up on them, he too became unhealthy.

Avoiding responsibility and blaming others are very common in both pain addiction and codependency. Blame greatly increases our problems with pain. When we blame, we act out our belief that the world is being run poorly by someone else. We avoid our responsibility. When we complain about our problems, we are rarely honest about the whole story, including our failures. Unfortunately, if we become chronic blamers, we may also feel compelled to persuade others that the way we see the world is right, while the way they see it is wrong. In short, if we deny our problems and if we blame, we don't take personal responsibility. In this condition we pass on our problems to other people, just like the pain addict.

Denying

People find many ways to adjust to pain. Denying reality is a common course. Some people learn to tune out pain in others. Unfortunately, this can cause the pain victim to pursue extraordinary and unhealthy means of gaining attention wherever he can. His unhealthy behavior only increases.

One of my closest friends, who had enjoyed a long and notable ministry, died a slow, agonizing death from liver cancer. Many times Christians greeted him with a smile. "I know God is going to heal you," they encouraged him. These would-be helpers could not deal with my friend's agony, so they avoided it by declaring it gone. At that point, they were not in a position to honestly minister to the family's pain and impending grief.

We don't like suffering and pain, so we adjust to it by declaring it "all better," or we deny it so we don't really have to deal with the issue.

Effects of the Relationship

The infectious quality of pain addiction is at the core of codependency. Codependency can take a toll on the pain addict's friends, family, and coworkers—in short, anybody who is in proximity. The more intense the pain addict's problem and the longer you are exposed to it, the greater the chance it will affect you. You can hardly live in a cage with a tiger and not get scratched. Codependency can cause a wide variety of serious emotional and physical problems.

One woman grew up in a family where both parents overate as a way of dealing with stress. This problem caused her great embarrassment while growing up. As an adult, she wanted so badly to be thin that she began to diet compulsively and finally became anorexic. She now teaches her children to control everything they eat—both as to quantity and type of food. Life in the dining room has been hard on these kids as they struggle to keep their mother happy. Instead of getting healthier, the kids are starting to have their own problems with compulsive overeating, anorexia, and bulimia. The pattern of pain avoidance behavior is often passed across generational lines.

Helping pain addicts can be hazardous to your emotional health. Coaddiction not only occurs when we live in the shadow of a pain addict, but also when we try to help them. We can't arbitrarily protect people from their pain or their problems, including those that result from their attempt to avoid pain. In the best case we get stressed out. In the worst case our efforts to help them out backfire. Their problems increase, we are unappreciated, and our relationship with them takes a turn for the worse.

Still, who has not tried to change a pain addict's behavior? Sometimes we do it out of benevolence. Other times we are motivated by desperation or frustration. All of us have spent time with a friend, coworker, or family member who has a problem with depression, alcohol, verbal and physical abuse, overeating, poor motivation, anger, or another mood-changing problem. If we're around these people for very long, we are tempted to convince them to mend their ways. We may use warnings, encouragement, challenges, confrontation, advice, or even bargaining to get them to alter their behavior. On occasion we may even have some temporary success. Long-term change, however, seldom occurs.

"Wait a minute!" you may say. "Aren't Christians supposed to help those in trouble?" Of course, but simply to get involved in others' problems is not always to help them. Trying to control their problems instead of allowing God to bring real change only makes the problem worse. There are times we must let go and let God change their lives.

However, staying free from codependent relationships with pain addicts is not as easy as it sounds. Our involvement often develops so slowly that we fail to notice the shape our relationship with the addict is taking.

Getting started in a codependent relationship is easy. We may see a friend spending way too much money. Anyone can see disaster is just around the corner. The solution appears obvious: He needs a more effective budget. We convince ourselves we merely have to voice our concern and willingness to help. The pain addict usually responds in one of two ways—like a tiger or like a lamb.

He may defend himself like a tiger to avoid facing a problem he's afraid he can't control. He may comply like a lamb if he believes his renewed effort with your help is finally going to fix his problems, or even that you may eventually assume some responsibility for his problems.

The Tiger

What happens if you try to help the tiger? This pain addict doesn't want his problems addressed no matter what toll they may be taking on himself or you. This pain addict growls or avoids you the moment you say anything about his problem behavior. The harder you try to discuss the problem, the worse his frustration becomes.

I remember an evangelist who cornered a friend of mine who had been talked into coming to church for the first time. I remember this pain addict (I'll call him Chuck) for two reasons. First, Chuck was given to alcohol and materialism. Second, he had a classic black 1958 Chevy Impala with custom diamond tuck upholstery and a souped-up engine and drivetrain. Chuck was pretty tentative about being in a church. He wasn't really ready to deal with either Christianity or his problems.

The visiting evangelist was determined to break through. He pushed harder and harder to get Chuck to become a Christian. By the time the service was over, it had become personal. People stood in the background and watched this battle of wills. The tension mounted. "Why don't you just accept the Lord now with all of these people watching—you may never get another chance?" the evangelist asked. Chuck held his tongue and finally escaped to the parking lot. I can still remember the smoke pouring from the Impala's rear tires. I never saw him at church again.

If you push the tiger, you may lose him to the church, you may lose him as a friend. Furthermore, after encountering an angry tiger, you may choose never to go back into the jungle. You might be tempted to quit trying to help anyone. "I'm never going to have anything to do with anyone like that again!" I hear people say.

The Lamb

The lamb, on the other hand, is usually quick to talk frankly about his problems. He makes it easy for you to become involved. In fact, he will respond in a positive way to almost anything you suggest. If finances are his problem, the lamb will be happy to take your suggestions to start a new budget. But a new budget doesn't stop the compulsive spending that created the problem. The compulsive spending remains unaddressed.

After talking with the lamb, you may feel you're making real progress in addressing his problems. It becomes very natural to get more involved, hoping to permanently improve his financial situation. "This time I know he will follow the budget—he promised me," you confidently say. But such dreams are rarely realized.

We cannot provide the pain addict with a way of fixing addictions, because we cannot control what the pain addict cannot control. Trying to control compulsive behavior without addressing the issues of addiction and pain avoidance is very much like pushing a wet noodle across a plate: The noodle never ends up in the right place.

By the time we have involved ourselves with pain addicts, our own ability to function is often affected and we find ourselves buying in to some of the compulsive person's reasoning. We are in too deep to get a proper sense of direction. We may start to become frustrated, still trying to figure out how to help the other person. But nothing we do can erase the problem. Consequently, we become further involved—we become codependent.

Whether the pain addict responds like a tiger or a lamb, his helper, the codependent, is in for a difficult time. Usually, the helper will get frustrated at the addict for having taken advantage of his good intentions. When this happens, the helper's first instinct is to stop caring or offering assistance. But that isn't the answer either.

When It's in the Church

Many know ministers who have interrupted their busy schedules to work with an alcoholic who arrives at the church on a Saturday evening wanting help. The alcoholic appears to be willing to change his life-style. He is compliant, courteous, and eager to participate and find employment. The minister finally talks a parishioner into providing him a job to begin Monday morning. The church dips into its funds to buy some acceptable clothes. The family of the youth director provides the alcoholic temporary lodging. Sunday morning is wonderful. The alcoholic looks and acts like a new man.

Come Monday morning at eight, when work starts, however, the alcoholic does not arrive. He has been passed out behind the bus station since three in the morning. The minister and congregation will never see him again. Consequently, they will be less eager to help the next alcoholic.

This is a classic case of codependency by members of the church. The alcoholic, although responsive, well-intentioned, and partially detoxed, simply was not in a condition to pursue a radical change of life-style. Still in early withdrawal (critical withdrawal usually will not even take place in the first twenty-four hours), in a partial blackout, and with a high degree of brain toxicity, he could neither think nor remember clearly what he was doing.

The minister related to the alcoholic as though he were simply a needy person with all his mental resources intact, rather than a pain addict. He was convinced the alcoholic, as a new believer, was now in control of himself; he would certainly make it back into a healthy life-style "this time." But barring a miracle, without proper detoxification and treatment, few alcoholics will stay sober, no matter what their first intentions are.

The alcoholic's upsetting visit to the church may result in two scenarios. The minister may simply swallow his frustration and embarrassment and determine to do better next time. As a result, his stress level will go up. Or the minister may decide against helping the next alcoholic who comes along. Both responses are codependent. Running from the pain addict is as much codependency as running to him. In both cases the unhealthy pain avoidance of the alcoholic has been passed on to the minister and others. Both the alcoholic and the minister have tried to fix a long history of addictive pain evasion with simple goodwill. Both pay a price. The minister becomes a bit more codependent, and the alcoholic remains dependent on the behavior that allows him to avoid the pain in his life. It is just too difficult for him to stop drinking. He is not really ready.

When It's in the Family

As damaging as codependency may be in a church setting or with friends, it can be worse in a home, because family members live so close together. If one member of the family is a pain addict, other family members can hardly escape the unhealthy behavior. The others in the family must find their own way to cope.

If, for instance, the father is violent and abusive, other family members may build their whole lives around appeasing, avoiding, anticipating, or otherwise trying to control his abusive patterns. But since an abusive person is never in constant control of his feelings, he is unpredictable. Family members may find it impossible to foresee his next action. Children are especially affected by this uncertainty.

Children from dysfunctional, addictive families often grow up to find they have great difficulty trusting their feelings, trusting others, and even feeling good about themselves. Statistics reveal they are vulnerable to depression, to addiction, and especially to passing their unstable life-style patterns on to their children.

"Family members need to detach themselves from the pain addict. Detachment doesn't mean they quit caring and helping in appropriate ways; it only means they quit trying to fix and control the other person's behavior."

What can the family with the abusive person do? Sadly, neither his family's genuine love and concern nor their fearful response are really much help. There are no easy answers.

Still, there is hope. First, they must let go of their assumption that they must—or can—solve the pain addict's problem. Not only do they need to turn the problem over to God, they need His help in relinquishing control before they make the problem any worse. Only God can tell us when to challenge and when to be supportive.

Family members need to detach themselves from the pain addict. Detachment doesn't mean they quit caring and helping in appropriate ways; it only means they quit trying to fix and control the other person's behavior. They must begin to keep a healthy emotional distance from the pain addict's problems.

Consider the classic case of the woman married to an alcoholic husband. She prepares a wonderful dinner and has it on the table at six—the time he said he would be home. An hour later everything is cold and she is furious. There will be a big blowup when her husband comes home.

But suppose the woman maintains healthy detachment. She simply goes on with her life, realizing her husband is not a well man and realistically he may not show up. At six she still has dinner on the table. Without being upset, she spends a pleasant meal with her kids, and she saves a plate for him in the oven in case he does come home. She goes on living. She knows she can't fix her husband's alcohol-related problem.

Detachment is not something we can achieve just because we

decide to do so. If we are already hooked in our relationship with the pain addict, periodically, if not frequently, we will be pulled into his problems. Many have decided not to get caught in an argument with a particular person when he or she is drunk. But, despite our best intentions, we get pulled in anyway. "Why won't you talk to me? I'm feeling so desperate to talk to someone right now," the person mumbles. "Just spend some time with me and I know I'll do better. You are a Christian aren't you?" By the time we get done explaining that he really needs detoxification, the whining and manipulation already have us under stress.

Warning Signs

Many warning signs can help you know if codependency may be developing in a relationship. Beware if you find yourself:

Demanding Change

There is a temptation to demand change in the addict's behavior even when it is obvious the addict is disinterested in change.

Remember, pain addiction by its nature is a problem that is always to some degree beyond the control of the addict. If we put pressure on the pain addict and convince him to change, he may react in two ways. First, he may try to change, only to fail. Second, he may simply deny his problem so he won't be able to fail.

Ignoring Stress-Causing Behavior

It can be tempting to try to live life as though the addict is not there, ignoring his behavior. This approach brings two problems: First, you may not be able to avoid the addict. Second, denying any problems in our lives—even if they start with someone else—is simply not wise. The secret to living around addicts is detachment—continuing to care and to stay involved but trusting God to keep you out of their control and under His control.

Becoming Angry and Resentful

Many people develop a habit of responding to stress by criti-

cizing the pain addict. But anger and resentment only perpetuate codependency. When we get angry with the pain addict, we
can fool ourselves into believing we are doing something to
bring about change. Anger gives us the mistaken impression we
are in control. Unfortunately, our anger rarely brings permanent change in the pain addict's behavior.

Giving Up

Frustration with a pain addict may cause us to give up and
quit caring. When children who were raised in homes dominated by a pain addict become adults, they often have the habit of
not following through with responsibilities and blaming their
problems on outside sources.

Manipulating

Some people attempt to manipulate the addict by drawing
attention away from the addict's problem. They may create projects or activities intended to keep the addict too occupied to
cause trouble. This strategy, too, is counterproductive. It merely
embroils us further in the pain addict's manipulation.

Accommodating

Those who adjust to or accommodate the pain addict may be
tempted to believe the problem they are avoiding is no longer
serious.

Families as a whole are easily damaged by accommodation.
Children especially may accommodate family problems by sub-
scribing to an unwritten code of silence. Nobody will talk about
the family's problem in order to avoid aggravating the pain
addict. But when the pain addict is accommodated, he will probably perceive this as a license to continue unhealthy behavior.

Another way we accommodate the addict is to make excuses
for his behavior in an attempt to protect him from criticism.
This wins points with the addict, but unfortunately we may
unintentionally begin to share his values, perceiving the world
in ways we know are unhealthy, contradicting our own value
system. In time, we may find increasing difficulty in sorting out
what is and isn't healthy in our relationship with the pain
addict. Since our addict friend isn't getting better, we may find

ourselves intimidated, on edge, constantly stressed, and uncertain of what to expect from the addict. We wonder when there will be more outbursts, blame, sullenness, and manipulation on the part of the pain addict.

Trying to Fix the World

Unfortunately, once we have learned to deal with a pain addict in an unhealthy way, it will be easier to begin drifting into unhealthy relationships with other pain addicts.

Why do we get pulled in? Sometimes we are overcome by our human drive to control pain, even if it is in others. Other times we try to help people because it makes us feel better about our image as servants, or helpers. And, on occasion, we minister not out of obedience to God, but in our personal effort to make the world (inclusive of alcoholics and other pain addicts) the way we prefer it to be.

Once we start trying to fix the world it is easy to lose perspective. We may begin to pursue our own agenda, deciding which hungry persons should be fed first, which alcoholics need counsel first, and even who should hear the gospel first. We may pour all our strength into one difficult case, only to see our efforts fail. Consequently, those we should have helped found us unavailable. We will find that when we minister by our own agenda, we will rock in the wake of everyone else's instability. Our effectiveness will only decrease with time because codependency, like any addictive response, is progressive. If we don't break free, we will get in deeper.

If we are caring people, we want to help those who hurt. But as we have noted, caring about others can invite trouble if we don't do it correctly. Not only can we waste our time and energy, but we also run the risk of inflicting damage upon the hurting person and ourselves.

In our attempt to make the world more positive, we may try to help someone else lose weight, quit smoking, stop being abusive, or even quit feeling depressed. "You can do it!" we tell them. But we forget what Jesus repeatedly said, "He who has ears, let him hear" (Matthew 13:43). We cannot force-feed recovery, and we cannot force people to face pain they're trying to avoid through alcoholism, overeating, rage, or anything else.

The tendency to try to change the world around us is strong

indeed. It is also codependent. It is right to help, to share joy, to challenge, and to bring change. As Christians we must bring real change in the economic, spiritual, political, and social contexts we find ourselves in. What we should not do, however, is attempt to bring about those changes in our own strength, wisdom, or timing. God will allow or bring change only according to His plan. His plan provides a crucial role for pain. Similarly, when we intervene in a person's life, it is imperative that we honor whatever role pain may be playing.

Allowing God to Work

I worked with a young alcoholic who had been in and out of churches. Dave had suffered from chronic depression and had been hospitalized repeatedly for mental problems. As he began another try at recovery, his first tendency was to stay busy and become very spiritual in an attempt to fight off impending depression and the drinking he knew would follow. He rose up early to study the Bible and pray. He went to extraordinary lengths to attend drug and alcohol meetings every day. He tried to stay sober with all his might, but every day he grew more fatigued. One afternoon he told me he sensed he was on the verge of losing it.

Patiently, step by step, I worked with Dave to help him slow down. As much as I wanted him to pray and study the Bible, I urged him to cut back his rigorous schedule. I encouraged him to take time off. Dave had to learn to trust God for his righteousness, rather than his own devotional efforts. He had to quit running from his pain. After two weeks of slowing down, he reported to me that he was now trapped in depression. It was no surprise that Dave found depression waiting for him when he stopped. He was really hurting.

One evening Dave and I talked about this new problem. If Dave were to speed up again, he might temporarily break free of his emotional valley. If he accepted the valley he was in, he would simply have to wait until the pain began to ease. I pointed out that buying time was no real solution, and acknowledged that facing the pain was a real solution that wasn't easy. Nevertheless, I suggested the valley he was in was, in reality, the spiritual solution to his problem. God was bringing about a healing. Dave needed to allow God to complete the work.

"God meets us in valleys as well as on mountaintops," I encouraged. "The pain isn't going to get worse unless you fight it. As long as you're responsible, I will stick with you through it all. Let yourself hurt whenever you need to. You don't have to feel up. We'll just wait for it to get better. Keep on with your recovery program."

There was no pleasure seeing Dave hurt, but before I could help him I had to accept the role of pain in his life. I could not change what God had not decided to change. In addition, if my own state of mind or health in any way became dependent on Dave's progress, then I might feel stressed as I tried to speed the process along. In time, I might give up or deny my inability to change Dave by blaming him. He had to remain in God's hands—I told myself—not mine. Ultimately, Dave allowed God to help him back into recovery from his addiction.

It is seldom easy to allow someone else to continue hurting or to encourage them to start feeling pain when it is needed. Generally speaking, if we drive up to the victims of a traffic accident or encounter a hungry child, we should try to alleviate the painful situation. On the other hand, when we encounter an emotionally painful situation that is preventing a person from greater harm, we should strongly consider whether helping him escape is in his best interest. For example, if you offer an alcoholic food, shelter, and a warm shower, you may be providing him temporary relief. You may even save his life. But you may inadvertently shore up his resources so he can continue to drink. Your well-intentioned efforts may actually help to kill him.

Sometimes, on our own, it is difficult to know whether the pain addict needs to be helped or to be challenged. On some occasions God will clearly reveal the answer. Other times God will help us determine whether the pain addict is sincerely interested in allowing pain to play a proper role in his life. This is best evidenced by long-term, consistent effort, honesty, and responsibility on the part of the pain addict.

Suggestions for Coping with Codependency

Letting Go

On occasion we become trapped in relationships with people

who are critical, offensive, manipulative, or who forever find creative ways to cause us emotional pain.

We may overcome such pain by burying our hurt and anger while trying to take the high road of noble response or we may become a fountain of bitterness, anger, and resentment. Eventually either response can make us as unhealthy as the person we are trapped with.

What is the solution? Letting go. With God's help we can cease blaming, fixing, or controlling. Instead, we can change what God directs us and allows us to change. Then we can let the relationship run its course. Sometimes we need an outside perspective, sound counsel, or support. We can pray. If you find yourself absolutely stuck with a bad situation, then by God's grace, use it as a growth experience

Being Honest

Try to make a realistic assessment of how you are coping in response to past or present, unhealthy, or abusive relationships in order to discover if you might need to work on codependency issues. Do you find the following patterns interfering with your current relationships?

Blaming
Trying to be more noble or perfect to help the relationship
Being possessive or controlling
Blocking out your emotions
Suffering when it is uncalled for
Denying your own failures
Retaliating or giving emotional paybacks
Accommodating, rescuing, or otherwise enabling

Joining Support Groups

It sometimes takes a person who has been in long-term unhealthy or abusive relationships to know how painful and disabling they can be. A person involved in such a relationship may want to consider visiting a group to get support from people who have struggled with similar problems. There are an increasing number of such Christian self-help groups now available that use biblical principles for recovery.

Helping the Addict

When we are trapped with someone who is abusive or who has serious emotional or addictive problems, it may only be a matter of time before we find ourselves pursuing desperate, and occasionally reckless, solutions.

But the best way to help a loved one who is in trouble is not what you may expect. For instance, statistically, the most effective way to help an addicted loved one is to first get help for yourself, to begin to deal with any tendencies toward codependency you may have. Far too often an addict gets pushed into treatment or counsel by a caring but overeager codependent. But the addict, even if he improves, is often destined to return home to an exhausted, wounded, fragile family of codependents who still have an agenda. Chaos, confusion, and relapse are all too likely to follow.

The simple fact is that the more you let go, the more likely your friend or loved one will cease defending himself and face his own problems.

Finally, don't overlook the program for recovery offered in the final chapter of this book.

TWELVE

GOD'S PLAN
FOR RECOVERY

"Since we have been justified through faith, we have peace with God through our Lord Jesus Christ, through whom we have gained access by faith into this grace in which we now stand. And we rejoice in our sufferings, because we know that suffering produces perseverance, perseverance character, and character hope."

—Romans 5:1–4

TWELVE

God's Plan for Recovery

A Gift of Mercy

Addiction has a well-earned reputation as a relentless pursuer. Once anyone is trapped by a dangerous addictive behavior, the odds are clearly stacked against him. Indeed, any person struggling with a weight problem, a prescription drug habit, anxiety, or any other persistent behavior may begin to wonder if breaking free will ever happen. Fortunately, the answer is yes. By following a well-traveled escape route found in the Bible, one can recover.

While millions of alcoholics, addicts, and others refer to themselves as being in recovery, the term itself can be difficult to pin down. By recovery, some people mean they are coping with a troublesome habit pattern, while others are referring to long-term sobriety. Still others are talking about salvation itself. Whatever you may call it—restoration, renewal, recovery, or even deliverance—when God helps you with an unwanted behavior it is a miracle. Recovery from addictions is not automatic or easy. The answer lies in accepting the gift of God's mercy. By necessity, the addict must accept the life of faith.

In the community of recovering addicts and alcoholics the concept of recovery is well established and deeply personal. For them, the traditional idea of recovery draws on the following premises: First, we must allow God to be in charge of our lives, and, second, we cannot solve our problems by our own strength. Willpower works against recovery. We must surrender our problems. God must help us, and we need to let Him—or we will not survive. In summation, recovery must be based upon endless trust in God.

Perhaps the greatest obstacle to recovery lies in our fear of trusting God with our failed behavior. Our tendency is to try to fix our problems rather than to focus on help. When in trouble, we tend to choose any relief that will take the pressure off *and* leave our accustomed life-style untouched.

One day I received a phone call from a woman who was acutely addicted to cocaine. She said she was desperate for help. She was about to lose everything. "What should I do?" she asked. "I'm using way too much!"

As we talked, I discovered she was really looking for a better way to control her addiction. She wanted drugs, but not the problems that accompany them. I searched for a way to break through her denial.

"Getting off cocaine," I said, "won't depend so much on what you do, as who you are. It may sound strange to you, but you have to become a totally new person!"

I knew this woman was incapable of fixing her addiction. She didn't need a technique; she needed a total make-over. She needed the gift of recovery. But unless her heart changed, she would never see the need to avoid drugs, much less turn to God for help. Sadly, she was hurting but not yet ready for that kind of change.

At times all of us try to control our lives in order to fix our problems. But we can't control everything. The struggle to control compulsive behaviors creates what are known on the streets as control junkies. Control junkies are persuaded that just one more try or a little more effort will resolve their personal crisis.

The greatest challenge in finding recovery from addiction or compulsive behavior is not in accessing God's mercy. The real challenge lies in a willingness to give one's life away, while at the same time trusting God to replace it with a life of His own making.

Listen to the words of Jesus: "The kingdom of heaven is like a merchant looking for fine pearls: When he found one of great value, he went away and sold everything he had and bought it" (Matthew 13:46). Like salvation, recovery is free, but at the cost of our whole lives.

Trusting is a commitment. It is to let go of the control of our lives. It implies we will yield our lives to God no matter what difficulty comes our way.

If one day, like Job, you awake to find your possessions gone and your family destroyed, how would you respond as a Christian? You could say God simply wants you to believe or pray the problem away. You could say you have been unfairly treated. You could trust God completely with whatever He allows to happen to you, and respond the way He leads you.

The last response given is an example of recovery. Recovery is always a gift. It does not come because you are a spiritual giant, but because God in His mercy puts it within your heart to trust.

Continual Trust

I have often heard addicts who are new to a recovery program say, "You know I'm really working hard at recovery. I know God helps those who help themselves." I respond, "Wait a minute, that's not in the Bible. You're quoting Benjamin Franklin! The truth is that God routinely helps people who can't help themselves. Recovery is a gift. We can reject a gift, misuse it, and even lose it, but we can never earn it!"

Even nonaddicted Christians can get caught in the idea of self-empowerment!

Cheryl, a recovering alcoholic, had been sober for six years. One night she ran into Sam, a friend she had not seen for several years.

"How are you doing, Cheryl?" Sam asked.

"I'm sober now," smiled Cheryl. "You know I'm a recovering alcoholic, don't you?"

"What do you mean, 'recovering'?" he asked. "If you're a Christian, you're not an alcoholic anymore. If you're delivered, you're a whole new person in Christ. Alcohol should no longer be a problem for you."

"Wait a minute," responded Cheryl. "Are you forgiven and delivered from sin?"

"Yes, of course," Sam said.

"Do you ever sin or start to fall into old sinful habit patterns?" Cheryl asked.

"Well, sometimes," Sam admitted.

"So you constantly have to depend on God to help you?"

"Of course I do."

"Then if you are trusting God for your righteousness you're in recovery from sin," Cheryl responded. "Recovery is continuing to trust God with old habits of any kind!"

If you think about it, every Christian should consider himself in recovery. What serious Christian does not desire to live as righteously as possible? But the world's best Christians, unless they are already absolutely perfect are called to the same life-long growth in righteousness as is the recovering alcoholic. (See John 15:1–4.)

Supernatural Deliverance

What about supernatural deliverance? "Welcome to the 'Hour of Evangelism'" an announcer said through my car radio. "Today we will broadcast the wonderful testimony of a Hell's Angel. You will hear the story of a hopeless drug addict who was left to die in a garbage bin. You will hear of Jesus' wonderful power to save."

I like those stories as much as anyone. They make me thankful. But I worry when wonderful stories of deliverance are recounted on television and radio programs as though everyone is changed through such high drama. We must be careful not to stereotype the moving of God's Spirit. God doesn't deal with every person's troubles the same way.

As wonderful as they are, spectacular deliverances can lead us to look at sins of compulsion simplistically: "Just quit. Just say no. Just don't do it. Just trust God, and it will go away." Scripture records that for many people, months and even years of struggle, failure, change, and growth are as much God's will as instantaneous solutions. We may hear testimonies or read books describing personal stories of deliverance. But what is often neglected is the lengthy, painful chronicle of what happened, especially subsequent failures. Slow personal growth doesn't make exciting reading or sensational stories. You may hear of treatment success rates soaring as high as the 90 percentiles. But when you consider client screening, length of stay, varying standards, and populations, as well as other factors that affect treatment results, the dramatic statistics simply vanish. As David Wilkerson, who has seen many victories and failures with addicts, noted in the *Cross and the Switchblade:* "Certainly we cannot claim a magical cure for dope addiction."

A large proportion of acute addicts and alcoholics will die early or quit of necessity when their bodies can no longer take the abuse. A small percentage will one day suddenly walk away from their addiction for no apparent reason. The great majority of addicts however, will enter the lifelong road of recovery if they are ever to be free.

Seeing deliverance in very narrow terms can be dangerous. The truth is, there are many Christians attending church each week who still have closet problems with serious addictions or destructive habits. They go to church because they are desperately seeking help. Yet, they don't publicly confess their need for fear of embarrassment and criticism. They have tried countless ways to change their life-style, and still they can't. They just keep trying harder. They continue to pray and seek God for deliverance and help. They repeatedly ask for prayer, seek new cures, buy self-help books, or listen to another sermon in a desperate bid for freedom.

What is wrong? They are often assuming recovery is achieved, not received. They assume that recovery is based on a single dramatic moment and that they must be the major player. But recovery is not a quick fix. It may arrive as quietly as the morning dew or overwhelm us like a storm. It is what we do with recovery in the long-term that is most important. Like salvation, recovery has a specific beginning point, but is intended to last forever.

I have a good friend, Fernando, who is recovering from habits that ruled his life. He was dangerously homicidal and often running from the law. He destroyed his family and his friendships—everything that got in his way. Finally he became suicidal and his few remaining friends, sure he would become just another statistic, gave up on him.

Late one night Fernando went on a terrible drinking binge. He crawled into his mother's house where he collapsed. Hiding from the law, he was without medical help and almost died from kidney failure. After lying semiconscious for nearly a week, detoxing from alcohol, he finally started to improve. After several more days, Fernando was just strong enough to leave his mother's house and walk along a favorite trail on his tribal reservation. Having nowhere in particular to go, he just wandered. But this time on the mountain trail his life was forever changed. The spiritual darkness that had been his companion for so long lost its grip.

Days before, as he neared death, someone had told him about

salvation. It had not made any sense. Now, as he walked along
the trail, he suddenly grasped its meaning for his broken life.
Jesus was for real.

Peace and hope welled up in his heart. He cried out, "God,
help me! I want Your salvation!" A miracle happened. God gave
him a new heart in place of his old one, and the gift of recovery
from his addiction.

From that day on the trail my friend became a new person.
He is, as Scripture says, a "new creation." But the transforma-
tion on the trail was not the end of the story for Fernando.
Recovery was only the beginning of his experience with God.

Despite Fernando's powerful conversion experience, he was
still not a perfect person. He was not without scars and frailties.
He still struggled, grew, and failed like anyone else. But, to this
day, there is one thing he always makes sure he does right: He
leans heavily on God to keep him from using drugs and alcohol
whenever the temptation recurs. And it does. The years of
habits imprinted in his brain are always waiting to reawaken.
On occasion they stir—especially during long periods of stress—
and Fernando has to reach out to God again to keep from slip-
ping back into addiction.

Fernando has not had a drink in years, but he knows he cannot become complacent and self-confident. He knows the danger
of relapse still awaits him should he ever disregard his relationship with God.

Recovery for alcoholics like Fernando is like salvation for a
Christian. Salvation does not mean that in our lives here on
earth we will be totally free from our limits, habits, failures, or
that we will be exempted from wreckage we may have created.
Being a new person in Christ does not mean that habit patterns
imprinted in the lower brain will suddenly disappear and no
longer pull at us, or that the liver tissue destroyed while drinking will necessarily turn healthy again. Neither does it mean
that the little girl killed by the drunk driver will come back to
life because the drunk driver became a Christian. It does mean
we are forgiven, and because of His presence in our lives we are
empowered to bend to His will. Salvation is the certainty that
God will bring us through. Salvation holds us fast to the Good
Shepherd and calls on God's righteousness rather than our own.

Twelve-Step Programs

We need to address a difficult and all too familiar controversy. This controversy turns on how Christians should deal with twelve-step groups, such as Alcoholics Anonymous.

Most people who get help for serious addiction patterns do so through Alcoholics Anonymous or some other twelve-step program. In fact, the success rate of these programs is very high for those who take them seriously. As late as the 1960s, most addicts first sought the support they needed in the church, but that is simply not where the majority of addicts go for help anymore. In most cities, addicts pursue help through a wide variety of twelve-step programs for gambling, eating disorders, co-dependency, alcohol, drug abuse, anger, and various emotional problems.

If millions of people are being served by the self-help groups, why do they make many Christians uncomfortable? The decades-old controversy for Christians stems from two issues. First, while some twelve-step support meetings are specifically Christian, many are not. Second, although each of the twelve steps reflects a scriptural truth, none of them spells out the gospel as it specifically relates to Jesus. This fact leaves many Christians skeptical.

Should Christians with an addiction use twelve-step groups? Christians themselves have different points of view. Some opponents argue that Christians should get help only in a church. Those who support twelve-step programs point out how many Christians with addiction problems are helped by such meetings. I have good Christian friends who are very uncomfortable about twelve-step groups, and other Christian friends who found their salvation in such meetings and think everyone should go.

The debate has gone on for decades, but, believe it or not, there are now some bridges being built between the two positions. A growing number of churches are addressing this controversy by starting Christian twelve-step meetings. In addition, several Christian recovery groups and numerous Christian treatment programs work alongside the traditional twelve-step groups using the same or slightly different steps.

Whether or not a Christian decides to join a twelve-step group is a personal matter. If you do decide to use such a group, you may want to ponder these suggestions:

Don't Expect People To Be Perfect

You will run into every kind of person in twelve-step groups; some will be wonderful, and others may be obnoxious. In addition, many kinds of twelve-step groups exist. Some are specifically Christian, but most are oriented to all comers. From the first days of the twelve-step tradition in the 1930s the idea was to take addiction outreach to the streets and to reach addicted people however possible, wherever they were, in whatever condition they were. They were not required to become Christians before they could receive help. Ideally, most churches operate in a similar fashion. People are allowed to arrive in whatever condition and with whatever understanding they have of the gospel. It is assumed that exposure to truth will bear fruit in God's time.

Use the Twelve Steps as They Reflect Scripture

The original twelve steps were never designed to replace the gospel; rather, they were to turn people to God. They were designed to reach drunks who weren't ready to listen to the "Four Spiritual Laws."

Time has brought changes. Over the decades many individuals and groups have joined the self-help (twelve-step) bandwagon, some having no interest in the gospel at all. In fact, they often take the twelve steps in a direction they were never designed to go. This type of diversion is not unique to twelve-step programs.

Churches, just as twelve-step groups, have those who try to pressure leaders to set a different spiritual agenda. Of course, the many cults, heresies, and strange doctrines that appear in some churches do not invalidate the message of the true Church. The tainted should never keep us from fellowship or ministry or even self-help groups.

It can be difficult for Christians to know what to listen for and what to be careful of, whether in a church or in a twelve-step meeting. Christians need to be discerning. Whenever you visit a new church, listen to a religious broadcast, or go to any twelve-step group, make sure the message is true to the Word of God. You will certainly hear both good and bad theology in twelve-step groups. So we should ingest spiritual teaching just like we do cherries—enjoy the fruit, but discard the pits.

Examine Your Reasons for Going

There are two important reasons why so many recovering Christians go to twelve-step meetings in addition to attending church. First, they receive valuable support from others who understand addiction patterns and have proven track records of recovery. Second, they go to share their faith even as they are receiving support.

What a place to share faith! Thousands of recovering addicts in twelve-step groups have come to trust God and have a deep hunger for the gospel. If no Christians went to twelve-step meetings and shared their knowledge of Scripture, the loss to God's kingdom would be great. For those Christians who have a heart for troubled people, those who identify with and love the addicted person, there is no richer field of service.

Look for Church Support

Many twelve-step groups meet in churches. Some use the traditional twelve steps and some use steps with evangelical terminology. In any case, the recovery principles are usually similar.

Be Honest

If you are a churchgoing Christian with an addiction problem that is not going away, get help. With some problems, failing to ask for help can be fatal. If you don't find help in the church from someone who understands your problem, don't give up on your church. Go to a twelve-step meeting and ask a Christian in recovery to sponsor you. He or she will help you get started in recovery.

Steps to Recovery

The AA Twelve Steps are designed to change lives. In fact, one of the biggest surprises addicts discover is that the steps barely address drugs or addictive behavior. What they do address are scriptural principles for change.

Let's take a short trip through the AA Twelve Steps and a simple application of them as they relate to problems of addiction, depression, anger, or any form of pain addiction. This application is meant only as an introduction.

Before we look at the twelve steps, however, one very important issue must be addressed. Anytime we see an arrangement of steps toward a goal, our first thought may be that we can use them to obtain what we want. If we have a problem with addiction, we may approach the twelve steps as a systematic way out. That isn't exactly how the twelve steps work. As with salvation, recovery is a gift from God and cannot be earned. There are no steps to earn salvation. Similarly, the twelve steps are designed to flow out of God's gift of recovery, not into it, which may be the reason they have been written in the past tense.

Step 1: "We admitted we were powerless over alcohol [pain, life's problems, sin, food, whatever it is that is controlling your life]—that our lives had become unmanageable."

"For all have sinned and fall short of the glory of God" (Romans 3:23).

This simple statement points out that we cannot control our problems. Until the law of pain is removed by God, we will never be able to manage our lives to escape the damage of pain. We cannot control our own destiny, and until we come to terms with that fact we will tend to manage our own lives, sometimes to the point of destruction.

Step 2: "[We] came to believe that a Power greater than ourselves could restore us to sanity."

"On him we have set our hope that he will continue to deliver us" (2 Corinthians 1:10).

This is one of the toughest of the twelve steps—even though most Christians subscribe to it. Why is it so tough? Although intellectually we may acknowledge that it is God who makes us new, living that conviction is more difficult. We are prone to solving our own problems, fighting our own war with pain, and inadvertently trusting in our own strength. Not that we want to depend on ourselves, not that we mean to, we just do.

Step 3: "[We] made a decision to turn our will and our lives over to the care of God as we understood Him."

"If anyone would come after me, he must deny himself and take up his cross and follow me" (Mark 8:34).

What is meant by "God as we understood Him"? God involves himself personally in our lives. That personal relationship is absolutely essential.

The writer of the AA Twelve Steps left Step Three less precise because AA reaches many people who would never go to church and have never read the Bible. Countless people in AA have responded to the third step and, in so doing, have come to know the full gospel.

Too often, people who are deep into addictions are at war with the world. They approach faith with a false cultural stereotype of God. They may well reject Him before they ever listen to Him. Often in working with people addicted to a habit, I encourage them to set aside their preconceptions and just ask the God of Scripture for help in whatever simple way they can, in whatever way they understand Him. I know God will answer their prayer. Sure enough, they soon come to know the living God!

Step 4: "[We] made a searching and fearless moral inventory of ourselves."

"Examine yourselves to see whether you are in the faith; test yourselves" (2 Corinthians 13:5).

This is a crucial step. First, it gives us a clearer sense of where we are in life and what we need to work on. Second, it keeps us aware of *Step 1.*

We must face the task of being utterly honest about our limitations and failures. Most people who do this step find, to their surprise, that they fill several pages with self-inventory.

Step 5: "[We] admitted to God, to ourselves, and to another human being the exact nature of our wrongs."

"Therefore confess your sins to each other and pray for each other so that you may be healed" (James 5:16).

"Wait a minute," we may protest. "I'm suffering from depression and I'm the one who has been hurt. Why should I worry about having hurt someone else?" Scripture makes it clear that we have all failed. That means we need forgiveness for failures we have long hidden. We need forgiveness for forgetting to love others when we have been distracted by our pain.

Step 6: "[We] were entirely ready to have God remove all these defects of character."

"Whoever believes in him is not condemned, but whoever does

not believe stands condemned already because he has not believed in the name of God's one and only Son" (John 3:17–18). Most of us want God to remove our faults, at least in theory. But fully and completely? Every last one? Now that's a difficult step!

Step 7: "[We] humbly asked Him to remove our shortcomings."

"I tell you the truth, unless you change and become like little children, you will never enter the kingdom of heaven" (Matthew 18:3).

We ask Him to form us into a new person. Again, the gift of recovery is not dependent on our sweat and strain; it is based on our willingness and faith.

Step 8: "[We] made a list of all persons we had harmed and became willing to make amends to them all."

"Therefore, if you are offering your gift at the altar and there remember that your brother has something against you, leave your gift there in front of the altar. First go and be reconciled to your brother; then come and offer your gift" (Matthew 5:23–24).

This exercise implies our willingness to take responsibility for failures and to try to bring healing where there has been hurt and wreckage.

Step 9: "[We] made direct amends to such people wherever possible, except when to do so would injure them or others."

"If your enemy is hungry, give him food to eat; if he is thirsty, give him water to drink" (Proverbs 25:21).

As God leads and helps us, He teaches us to take responsibility for our failures rather than blaming them on others. Blaming ourselves or others for failure yields nothing constructive. Taking responsibility brings healing.

In addition, we need to ask forgiveness and to reconcile past debts and wreckage.

Step 10: "[We] continued to take personal inventory, and when we were wrong promptly admitted it."

"So then, each of us will give an account of himself to God" (Romans 14:12).

We must never lose touch with our limitations and failures. To forget our failures is to turn to self-righteousness and to cease depending on God for our righteousness.

Step 11: "[We] sought through prayer and meditation to

improve our conscious contact with God, as we understood him, praying only for the knowledge of His will for us and the power to carry that out."

"If my people, who are called by my name will humble themselves and pray and seek my face and turn from their wicked ways, then will I hear from heaven and will forgive their sin" (2 Chronicles 7:14).

Because we cannot direct our lives successfully, we must utterly trust God's direction. It is by His strength that we break the power habits have on our lives and begin to face and process our everyday pain.

Step 12: "Having had a spiritual awakening as the result of these steps, we tried to carry this message to alcoholics and to practice these principles in all our affairs."

"Always be prepared to give an answer to everyone who asks you to give the reason for the hope that you have" (1 Peter 3:15).

We must have a real experience with God if we hope to share faith with others. I had a good friend who has long since gone to be with the Lord. I personally know of her leading hundreds of addicted people to the Lord! Brenda had grown up in the home of a pastor but had wandered into a life of debauchery and drunkenness. When she finally tried to quit drinking, she failed time and again. No matter how much she tried or prayed, she couldn't seem to avoid alcohol. She was completely addicted.

It was in the early days of Alcoholics Anonymous in Los Angeles. Things were pretty bad for her. Her phone seemed to be silent for days on end. She felt alone, like nobody in the whole world cared. Across town was Tim, who had just become sober through Alcoholics Anonymous. He was eager to share his newfound freedom.

Brenda's phone rang one day. "Hey, Brenda, this is Tim. Why don't you come over and I'll fix you breakfast?" Brenda's defenses went up as quickly as she recognized his voice. *Something is going on,* she thought. *Tim is a jerk and wouldn't fix breakfast for anyone.* To her surprise she answered, "I'll come right over."

Brenda never forgot walking into Tim's house that morning. As she stepped through the door, she felt the awesome presence of God. Not a word was spoken, but she suddenly began to weep. In that moment the truth took root in her heart. She would never drink again. Brenda's recovery, as with most alcoholics, was a long, difficult road, but she held on, one day at a time. Periodically, from nowhere, the urge to use would come back (spontaneous recovery), but every time she "worked the steps" and God helped her through it. For twenty-six years she served in public ministry, reaching out to people in the church and in Alcoholics Anonymous.

Perhaps you have heard recovering alcoholics refer to themselves as grateful alcoholics. They are not grateful for the pain they have caused others; they are merely saying they are grateful to have a problem with alcohol because it forces them to depend on God and, hence, to obtain recovery and the gift of a new life.

No matter what the emotional pain is in your life, no matter what the thorn is in your heart, there is hope; first in understanding the pain, then in facing it and allowing God to apply His gift of mercy. For ultimately it is the One who wore the thorns who can remove the thorns.